W9-DAH-235

THE POOR OF THE EARTH

[handwritten inscription]

Geneva
Switzerland

May 1976

The Poor of the Earth

JOHN COLE

© John Cole 1976

All rights reserved. No part of this publication may be
reproduced or transmitted, in any form or by any means,
without permission

First published 1976 by
THE MACMILLAN PRESS LTD
London and Basingstoke
Associated companies in New York
Dublin Melbourne Johannesburg and Madras

SBN 333 19518 3 (hardcover)
SBN 333 19519 1 (paperback)

Printed in Great Britain by
UNWIN BROTHERS LTD
Woking and London

The paperback edition of this book is sold subject
to the condition that it shall not, by way of trade
or otherwise, be lent, resold, hired out, or otherwise circulated without the publisher's prior consent
in any form of binding or cover other than that in
which it is published and without a similar condition including this condition being imposed on the
subsequent purchaser.

This book is sold subject
to the standard conditions
of the Net Book Agreement

Dedicated to my Father and Mother

Contents

Preface

What will the world be like in the year 2000? Futurology concerns itself mainly with the blessings or dangers of scientific discovery. But there is a more basic aspect of the final quarter of our century with which I believe intelligent people ought to concern themselves. This is world poverty, the ability or otherwise of the rapidly growing population of this planet to feed, clothe and house itself.

Acute international political controversy surrounds this subject. For years the Third World has been agitating for what it calls a New International Economic Order, and while I was writing this book, that concept of international co-operation to solve the problems of poverty received a more general blessing at the Seventh Special Session of the United Nations General Assembly in New York. In the world in which we live, that counts as progress, but I fear it will be an empty gesture, and that the New Order will not help the poor much more than the Old Order did, unless we take greater care about two controversial ingredients of development strategy, employment and income distribution.

This book is an attempt to examine these matters. Its thesis is that we can only hope to have a prosperous and happy world when proper work has been provided for hundreds of millions of people who today either have no jobs or else perform work which is not sufficiently productive to support them and their families.

The book was conceived during a visit to the International Labour Organisation in Geneva in the spring of 1975. Preparations were then beginning for a great international gathering, which the ILO had decided to sponsor in the summer of 1976. To give this its full title, it is the Tripartite World Conference on Employment, Income Distribution, Social Progress and the International Division of Labour. It is more briefly called the World Employment Conference.

Since 1969, the ILO has been busy with a World Employment Programme, which is its contribution to the United Nations' Second Development Decade, covering the seventies. One aspect of this programme is research into unemployment and underemployment in the Third World, and the complementary adjustment problems in the richer countries. In many poor nations, unemployment is only the tip of an iceberg, though the figures for even that are startlingly worse than in the rich countries. But the major cause of gross poverty, both in the countryside and the cities, is the prevalence of work which barely produces enough to keep body and soul together.

The ILO and other international bodies have many technical assistance projects intended to help with such problems. But one of the most significant developments in recent years has been the assembling by the ILO of seven national employment missions. These have studied the economies of individual countries in the Third World, and offered advice to their governments. The reports of these missions form a new corpus of knowledge about development strategy. In the summer of 1975, I followed in the footsteps of three of the missions — to Kenya, Sri Lanka and the Philippines — to see how their reports had been received.

Any traveller in the Third World is struck, as I have been in the past, by the obscene contrast between the poverty he sees around him and the comparative wealth of the developed nations. But there is another, equally obscene contrast: between the privileged groups in almost every developing nation — and that often includes not only the conventionally rich, but many workers in their modern industries — and the masses of the poor. The theme of this book is the strategy which is now emerging to tackle these complementary obscenities. I am convinced — as are many specialists in international development — that neither can be solved if the other is ignored.

This book is not addressed to development experts. It is

designed to open up one of the most important human and political controversies in the world today to the man in the street, whether he be politician, civil servant, industrialist, trade unionist, academic, student, or just an intelligent observer of the human condition. In preparing it, I have been given unstinted help and advice by men and women in Geneva, London, Washington, and in the Third World, who are devoting their lives to the alleviation of world poverty. I have drawn freely on their conversations and writings, and ask that this be taken as a general acknowledgement, as the sources are too numerous to list.

Some of them will be infuriated as they read this book, believing that I have over-emphasised the selfishness and inadequacy either of rulers in the Third World or of the West. In hope of disarming such criticism, it may be worth describing the shape of the book. In the first two chapters, I have sketched out the scale and background of world poverty, and explained what I have called the two obscene contrasts. There follow three chapters reporting on the particular problems of Kenya, Sri Lanka and the Philippines. Then come three further chapters dealing with what is being done, or needs to be done, in the rural areas and cities of the Third World.

When he has read that far, the reader in the West may be tempted to sit back, in the complacent belief that if only the fat cats in the developing countries would forget their windy rhetoric, and instead display a little less greed, and even venality, their poorer neighbours would be better off. But in the remaining chapters, which examine the international dimension, I hope that such complacency will be dispersed. For if the poor of the world are to have a chance to support themselves in greater decency, much will be required of the richer nations, including freer trade and a steady restructuring of their industries, so that work in which the developing countries have a comparative advantage can be transferred to them. If we are morally incapable of facing this challenge during the remainder of this century, it will be a poorer world in more than the purely economic sense.

Claygate, Surrey   J.C.
October 1975

1 The Scale of World Poverty

The Third World has reached the end of its age of optimism. In the twenty years after the Second World War, as the countries of Africa and Asia moved, one by one, bloodily or peacefully, to independence, men hoped that with self-government would come prosperity, that development would gradually abolish poverty and malnutrition, and that the new countries would join the old ones, 100 or 150 years later, in progress towards decent living standards for the mass of their people.

It is not easy, in the rapidly curdling atmosphere of the fourth quarter of the twentieth century, to recapture the mood of the fifties and early sixties. Yet it was heady at the time. Recrimination about past relationships between colonial powers and the newly independent states seemed less important than the new start which was being made. Those people in developed countries who cared about the Third World had the comfortable feeling that at last their governments were doing the right thing, that a new era of equity and peace was beginning. And they wanted to help.

As for the leaders of the new nations, many of whom had suffered hardship, humiliation and imprisonment on the road to independence, their excitement was almost tangible. The raising of the new flag, the playing of a new anthem were both an end and a beginning. They might have echoed the lines of Wordsworth at the time of the French Revolution:

Bliss was it in that dawn to be alive, But to be young was very heaven.

As often happens in human affairs, the event has not lived up to the expectation. The wine of freedom has soured, just as it did during the French Revolution. This does not mean that independence was not right. But freedom has not brought prosperity. The masses of the Third World, in Asia, Africa and Latin America still exist in poverty. About half of them — 1000 million human beings — live in countries where the per capita income is less than $200 a year.

We are now entering a quarter-century in which the world will face recurrent food crises. Yet perhaps half of these 1000 million poorest people are already hovering on the verge of starvation, and some estimates suggest that 10 million are in imminent danger of death. But how, even, does one know whether such rounded statistics measure the actual perils of the world's poorest people, when a widespread drought or some other natural disaster, or the failure of a few key crops, in their own countries or in the Soviet Union and China, could kill far more?

Behind this gathering gloom is the fact that about 300 million human beings are either unemployed or have not found sufficiently productive work to maintain life above the poverty line. Before the year 2000, another 1000 million people may be added, by the increase in world population, to this roll-call of the desperate. Providing work for these people is the only way to alleviate the most crushing poverty.

The failure of expectations has produced both despair and anger. Internationally, it has sent the Third World and the rich countries of the West into a downward spiral of recrimination (from which the Communist countries, a little unctuously, exclude themselves). The West is critical of how the developing countries conduct their affairs. Too much creed, say some. Too much greed, others reply. The ruling élites of the Third World are seen as often corrupt, always too little concerned with the gross inequalities within their own societies. In reply, the West is charged with being restrictive in trade, mean in giving aid, and generally obstructive to the progress of the poorer nations.

Within the developing countries, failure in economic progress has produced political instability, frequent coups, a few terrible civil wars, the constant threat that new nations will break up into their constituent tribes, and a steady erosion of the Third World's infant democracy. As I write, the largest of the countries to secure its independence from colonial rule, India, has seen its liberties savagely curtailed by Mrs Gandhi's government.

Throughout the world it is now accepted that economic policies for most developing countries have either failed or will succeed so slowly that the prosperity, and in some cases the lives, of two or three generations would have to be sacrificed if their governments were simply to keep on their present paths and wait for results. This is not the moment to analyse what has gone wrong. That will be done, in passing, throughout this book. Although my principal purpose is to describe the ideas for a happier future which are now emerging, inevitably the failures of the past will have to be looked at.

What must be said at once is this: It is one of those recurring tragedies in man's affairs that, just at a moment when development economists and other experts may have hit upon a strategy which offers hope of a better life for thousands of millions of deprived people, the world shows every sign of missing the opportunity. Lest this book falls into the trap of optimism, I had better straight away set down my fear that the likeliest outcome of the next few years is an increasingly bitter atmosphere between the rich and poor countries, a crescendo of accusing rhetoric on either side, and a self-defeating confrontation about how to divide the existing riches of the earth, which will inhibit the creation of new riches that might give simultaneous prosperity to all.

Just at the moment when détente, now given the imprimatur of the Helsinki Declaration, takes the sharp edge off the quarrel between East and West which occupied the third quarter of this century, so a new and bitter quarrel is building up between North and South, the haves and have nots. It is all too probable that this quarrel will dominate world affairs till the year 2000, and its effects could be explosive. Man, it almost seems, is never at rest without some great international squabble to stop him thinking about his real problem — the long, grinding struggle against want.

It was in the late sixties that the optimism with which the newly independent countries had launched themselves began to evaporate. With hindsight, it is possible to see what they and the world did wrong. One disillusioned idealist, a Frenchman with a humane but questioning mind, suggested to me that the basic mistake of the Third World was to look at all at the model of the industrialised world and its consumer society. For him, the whole problem was encapsulated in a simple question: Is it worth working harder to get another gadget?

Others do not see it either so starkly or so pessimistically as that, but they argue that instead of studying industrialised countries as they are now, the Third World ought to have looked instead at the more relevant model of these countries at the time of their Industrial Revolutions. Economically, that is good advice. Psychologically, the direction initially taken by the new countries was inevitable. Under colonial rule, they observed — and envied — white men who had achieved a high standard of living because they belonged to industrialised and consumer-conscious societies. Nothing less was good enough for the new nations of black, brown and yellow men.

Therefore, concentrate on modern industry, on the prestige of the capital city, on the small, visible part of the population who live in towns, instead of the 50, 60, 70 or more per cent who struggle on for existence in the immemorial poverty of the countryside. Much political thinking in the new nations is dominated by fear that they will be cheated again, that their people will be left as hewers of wood and drawers of water for the privileged, and now distant, nations who formerly ruled them.

This fear is one reason for reluctance to rely too heavily on primary products. It explains the almost obsessive wish to have a white-collar job, however boring or non-productive. Interestingly, that desire was evident also among American blacks during the civil rights struggle. It probably grew out of a lingering suspicion that, as on the cotton and tobacco plantations of the Old South, the black man will always be left sweating in the fields, while the white man does something cerebral — in a white suit and wide-brimmed hat.

Even when economic sense points to different methods of production, old suspicions understandably die hard. Much will be said later in this book about labour-intensive methods. Economically, they are an important part of the drive for prosperity in the next decade or more. But, as one Third World economist wryly observed to me, the people who advocate them are nearly all economists and others who work with their brains rather than their hands.

One of the most quietly encouraging projects I saw on my travels was the building of a rural road in Kenya by methods that cannot have been used in Europe or North America for many years. Huge quantities of earth were being moved not by mechanical means, but by wheelbarrow. The digging was not done by the vast bulldozers of a Western building site, but by spade. It made sense because it employed people who had no hope of earning a cash income in any other way, it was economical, and it would provide a much-needed road between the workers' family farms and the market — which, again, they would not get in any other way. But when I heard that one of the principal uses of convict labour in colonial days in Kenya was to build roads, the initial suspicions about such labour-intensive methods again became comprehensible. White men used to make black men sweat at such work. Folk memories die hard.

So while the arguments which will rage in the next few years, and which are reflected in this book, are partly economic, partly political, it is wise never to forget that they have a psychological undertone. That is what shapes the battle now going on within the United Nations system. This battle will have tragic results for the world unless it is stopped, unless confrontation is replaced by co-operation.

A case can be made out, of course, for the belief that the Third World has no alternative but to confront the West aggressively. Have not the oil producers shown what can be done? Won't you only get justice when you seize it? Haven't the former colonial powers, who control the financial and trading systems of the world, continued to operate these in their own favour — over tariffs, commodity prices, exchange rates, and so on? And won't they continue to do so until they are forced to stop?

Yet reading the documents produced by the non-aligned group of nations for various UN conferences, one is struck not so much by the many practical demands, but by the aggressive rhetoric which clothes them. This is most noticeable when they mention the OPEC oil price increases. These increases have hit the poorest developing countries more severely than anyone else, both directly and because of the suffering caused to primary producers by the recession in the developed world. Yet there is positive enthusiasm for the OPEC action in the Third World.

This is not because those who wrote the documents see OPEC s action as a pattern for other producers; there is no commodity in quite such a strong position as oil. But the sight of the Western economy ravished by the actions of Third World countries has obviously fulfilled a psychological need. The poor nations like to see some of their number get up off their knees (as it appears to them), even if the result is injury to themselves as well as to the rich world. This attitude is not without precedent. People in occupied Europe during the last war used to cheer as British and American bombers devastated not only the defences of the Nazis, but also the homes of their own countrymen. Hate is often a stronger feeling than love. In London recently, a thoroughly rational Indian who has contributed much to good race relations in Britain, admitted that nothing has given him more pleasure than to see British ministers licking the boots (as he put it) of the Shah of Iran, the Saudi Arabian leaders, and others whose investments in London matter a lot in the present sickly state of the British economy.

The West also has its psychological hang-ups. In the UN organisations, the habitual majority which was once led by the United States has been eroded by the accession of new nations. Now there is a natural majority of the developing countries (including the comparatively rich oil producers) and the Communist bloc. On a whole series of resolutions to do with the proposed New International Economic Order, the developed countries have found themselves outvoted. Looked at from an American point of view, it seems that the richest country in the world is being ostentatiously insulted and at the same time being asked for generosity in its trade and aid policies.

At a time when all the developed economies are afflicted

by an unprecedented combination of inflation and unemployment — which was triggered off, if not caused, by the oil crisis of 1973 — this looked like driving America and at least some of her friends into the laager: a laager consisting of the organisations which they can still control, and in which they believe the real economic power of the world still resides — the World Bank, the International Monetary Fund (IMF), and the General Agreement on Tariffs and Trade (GATT).

To add irrelevant insult to injury, the long-running tragedy of the Middle East has cast its shadow over the UN. In agency after agency — UNESCO, the World Health Organisation, ILO, and the General Assembly itself — some issue concerning Israel has produced an angry flare-up between the Western world and the rest. It scarcely matters whether the issue is Israel's alleged treatment of religious shrines, its labour policies as they affect Arabs in the occupied territories, the admission of the Palestine Liberation Organisation as an observer, or the branding of Zionism as racism. American politicians, with their legacy from an age when their country was the melting-pot for European refugees, are as careful of the Jewish vote as of the Irish or Greek. Add to this the strong reek of hypocrisy in Third World attitudes to Israel, and the knowledge that Israel remains a democracy while many of her accusers are not, and you have a recipe for strife.

Hypocrisy lies also at the heart of the main argument. For there are two obscene contrasts in the world today. The one to which the Third World rightly draws attention is the contrast between the rich countries — including much of the Communist bloc — which contain something over 1000 million of the world's people, and the developing countries, which have more than 2500 million people already, and are expected to outnumber the developed world four to one by the end of the century.

But the fading conscience of the rich nations is not the only obstacle to help for the poorest of the poor. Within the developing countries themselves is to be found an equal obscenity in the contrast between the mass of the people, living in unchanged poverty, and the rich — the small, ruling élite, which controls government, industry and nearly all the wealth, owns most of the land, and appears as reluctant to countenance radical changes at home as it is vociferous in demanding them abroad.

Out of these two obscene inequities, the best hope lies in a trade-off. In this, the rich countries of the West would accept most of the Third World demands: liberalised trade, leading to a new international division of labour, with the poorer countries processing much more of their own raw materials, taking over industries which they can carry on more effectively than the West — textiles, clothing, footwear, and so on — and also receiving better and assured prices for their commodities and products.

In return, the rich and powerful governing groups within the Third World would have to agree to give their countries the only economic stimulus which will make them take off before the end of this century — a radical redistribution of income and wealth. The most inequitable spread of income in the world is in poor countries, those where the per capita income is between 100 and 500 dollars. To change this means land reform, greater concentration of effort and resources on agriculture and rural development, encouragement of small-scale industry in which poor people can make money, at the expense of large, modern, artificially protected industries which benefit those who are already well off.

At last countries like India, Kenya and Nigeria would have to face the fact that the greed and corruption which disfigures their political and commercial life denies hope to millions of starving or near-starving people; that self-generating development cannot be produced at the wave of an international wand, through better trading conditions from the West, new codes of conduct for multinational companies, or the sacrifice of jobs by workers in developed countries (necessary though these may be); and that only by spreading money out among the masses of their own population will they create the large home markets for their goods which will give their economies real strength.

This trade-off will not be easy to accomplish. The West's steps towards trade liberalisation are plodding and reluctant. On the other side, the Third World's conversion is equally slow. In the New International Economic Order, fathered by the non-aligned group in the United Nations, not much emphasis is placed on the need for redistribution of wealth within their own societies. Sceptics in the West say that this is because those who write such documents are drawn from their countries' privileged classes, who stand to lose by redistribution.

'Always remember', one radical Western expert advised me, 'that every African or Asian who attends an international conference is rich within his own society. He has a privileged position, a much sought-after job, a prosperous life, probably cushioned by servants. It explains a lot about attitudes.'

Whatever the reason, the whole emphasis in the New International Economic Order is on what others must do. Yet among development economists, income distribution has become an increasingly dominant theme, as they survey the wreckage of existing policies. In brief, these relied on creating a Western type of economy in the new countries. It was hoped that as modern industry developed it would create wealth to filter down to the poorer people, who mostly lived in the rural areas. Gradually they would be sucked into the labour market, as they had been at the time of the Industrial Revolution in the West.

These policies of the older development experts, supported by the national political élites, drowned the new voices which began to be raised in the late fifties and early sixties. Those who argued that a more direct attack on unemployment and underemployment was needed were given only a polite hearing in the United Nations and by world political leaders. The Alliance for Progress, covering the Americas, thought this was 'too revolutionary' an issue to tackle. The ILO could not get employment accepted as a key issue for the First Development Decade in the sixties. Growth was all, gross national product the god. So, until quite recently, it has remained. Only now is the ILO's chosen role as the world's conscience about its unemployed and underemployed acknowledged to be an important one.

The failure of development policies along traditional lines is sometimes blamed on restrictive trade policies in the developed world. The West's behaviour has certainly been a factor. It has concentrated too much on aid, and even in this has often been both niggardly in scale and selfish in the kind of aid it gave, seeking trade advantages and perpetuating a semi-colonial relationship. But even if there had been more enlightened trade and aid policies by the West, the Third World's development would have begun to sag in the sixties. It simply was not possible to reproduce the Industrial Revolution, which has spanned the eighteenth, nineteenth, and much of the twentieth centuries in Europe and North America, in one generation. This was particularly true against a pattern of wealth distribution which made the developed countries look positively egalitarian.

People like Robert McNamara, of the World Bank, and Louis Emmerij, of the ILO's World Employment Programme, have been nudging the world towards a new and more radical approach to development for some years. But there is a serious time-lag between such pointing of a timid finger, which is the most that international institutions can do about the mistakes in policy within member states, and the intellectual conversion of decision takers in developing countries.

McNamara has thrown the weight of the World Bank behind his belief that poverty and starvation must be attacked first through improvement of agricultural production in the Third World, and then by building up the small trades of the informal urban sector of the economy. Even if the food surplus countries produced enough to meet statistically the needs of the world, the hungriest people would not be able to buy the food they need. Yet few developing countries have a coherent policy for food production or an effective strategy for rural development. Their low output per acre is a major cause both of the world food shortage and of their own most devastating poverty. The food gap is getting worse rather than better.

In this and other fields, because Third World governments have followed too slavishly the developed economies, they have missed essential steps in their own progress. In many countries education has concentrated too much on prestige institutions of higher learning, which can only benefit a tiny proportion of the population, instead of teaching basic skills to the mass of the people. This, in turn, has often produced a new class of 'educated unemployed', who refuse to take jobs lower than those for which their education qualifies them. Too much effort is sometimes spent on their problem, and too little on the crushing poverty of those with neither education nor an adequate means of earning a living. The World Bank has given a warning that unless education is reformed to meet development needs, the Third World will enter the twenty-first century with its most productive resource, its people, 'badly prepared and doomed to live in poverty and ignorance'.

What brought the problems of employment and income distribution out into the open in the mid and late sixties was the realisation that the Third World was running very fast to stay in the same place, or even falling back. The unforeseen factor was the scale of the population growth. Not that the issue was new, but the censuses which began to appear at that time revealed on the horizon the galloping horseman of demography. The rate of population growth, mostly concentrated in the poor countries, had risen to 2 per cent. That would lead to a doubling of the total population of the world within thirty-five years. The previous doubling took about fifty years; the one before that one hundred and ten years.

Someone said that the problem was modern death rates combined with mediaeval birth rates. In a way, that is too comforting. Recent population growth has been concentrated in eight large developing countries – China, India, Indonesia, Brazil, Bangladesh, Pakistan, Nigeria and Mexico. With 1800 million people, representing 70 per cent of the population of the Third World, these countries added 600 million people to the human family between 1950 and 1970. They will add a further 950 million – more than half the world increase – in the next twenty years.

Yet all except three of these countries – Brazil, China and Mexico – have not yet achieved their modern death rate. Theirs are well above the world average, and even above that of the developing world. So they still have a long way to go; and assuming that their death rates can be substantially reduced, the growth in their populations will rise significantly in the future unless there is a sharp fall in their birth rates.

The days of easy solutions and easy optimism about population control have passed. Merely to distribute contraceptives and transistor radios now seems naive. People in poor countries have large families for a wide variety of reasons which seem good to them. One is an infant mortality rate which remains tragically high — 140 per thousand live births, compared with 27 per thousand in developed countries. So the problems of big families and poverty are connected, but it is not a simple matter of the former being the cause and the latter the effect — as many Western people, with the virtuous feeling of having produced only a small family, tend to assume. Low incomes and maldistribution of income contribute to high fertility rates; poor men look on their large families as rich men look on their insurance premiums. Only with development plans that help the poor can we hope to reduce the rate of growth in our population, and avert the spectre of a world getting more and more crowded and more and more poor.

The broad decisions which the international community ought to take are already clear. There must be significant increases in financial help to the Third World. As little as $.2000 million extra each year would give first aid to the very poorest countries, but much more is really needed. There ought to be changes in the kind of aid; it must come in the forms which will most help the developing country. This is best done when aid is channelled through the World Bank or another international institution, rather than in the self-interested form which bilateral, or country-to-country aid too often takes.

Then, the Third World also needs enlightened help to give it a system of technology which is tailor-made to its own needs rather than to the export industries of the West — small cultivators, ploughs, tractors and other agricultural implements; and simple rather than elaborate and expensive manufacturing machinery, which will encourage employment of its abundant labour, rather than suck up its scarce capital.

Finally, it needs a reduction in trade barriers and planned trade expansion, especially through a huge increase in the processing of raw materials in the Third World. This will affect employment in the richer countries. But as many as twenty jobs could be created in the very poorest countries for the loss of one job in the United States or Western Europe.

Such changes will be difficult to achieve, difficult to conceive even, in the middle of a world depression. Yet what those of us who live in the rich countries and are obsessed with our own problems ought at least to know and remember is that between a quarter and a third of the people in the Third World suffer from a poverty whose depths we can scarcely imagine.

Their own rulers and countrymen ought to remember that also. Some of them are beginning to be sensitive to the gross inequities, as well as the gross poverty, in their own countries. A well placed observer said recently:

I'm less pessimistic now. Look at President Marcos in the Philippines. He wants to stay in power, so he's going against his own personal wishes and bringing in reforms just to stay on top. Perhaps only he, and not a Left-wing leader, could get away with some of the things he's doing.

More and more politicians in the Third World see the writing on the wall. They see that if they don't reform their countries, they'll finish up on a lamp-post. Much of the rhetoric surrounding the New International Economic Order, all that talk about wicked capitalists, is just to divert attention from poverty, to buy them a breathing space. The pressure is on, and even the corrupt politicians know it.

But I don't feel at all relaxed about the situation. The West needs to come up with a new Marshall Plan, one that is both generous and realistic in our relations with the poorer countries. If we did that, we could afford to bring pressure on the Third World about their internal policies. But if we can't produce a grand design of some kind, there'll be an explosion within ten or fifteen years.

2 The Trade-Off

I have described the gulfs in prosperity between the developed and developing countries, and between the rich and poor within the Third World as obscenities. We could, however, be in process of creating a third offence to human decency which would be almost as obscene. That would be if the two sides in the current quarrel between the two worlds allowed it to escalate so much that they failed to find the necessary compromise, and thus allowed the world to slither into a running, pseudo-ideological struggle in which everyone would suffer but the poor would suffer most of all.

'Pseudo-ideological', because a kind of mock battle is now developing between planners and free market advocates, capitalists and socialists. At most the ideology is woolly and the differences are blurred at the edges. More often the whole argument is overlaid with hypocrisy or cynicism, with words not used to mean what they appear to mean. Someone once said unkindly of an Indian intellectual that if he came upon two doors, one marked 'heaven' and the other 'discussions about heaven', he would choose the latter. The tendency is not confined to India, nor to the Third World.

The hair-splitting and political posturing which go on among the West, the Communist bloc, and the Third World are understandable. It is too easy to become angry, rather than concerned, about world poverty, to see the other man's faults rather than one's own, as one of Christ's Parables observed. The danger in the next few years, and particularly at the World Employment Conference, is that each side will point an accusing finger at the other; that everyone will call on everyone else to play his essential part in reform; and that no one will actually do anything which is inconvenient to his own interest or country.

When set against the plight of 800 million of the poorest people in the world, such a sham fight is offensive. As Robert McNamara said, most of these people, representing 40 per cent of the Third World population, are trapped in their poverty, hardly surviving on the margin of life, in conditions so degraded by disease, illiteracy, malnutrition and squalor as to deny them the basic human necessities. They are neither contributing significantly to their nations' economic growth nor sharing equitably in their economic progress.

In the past few years, the countries to which these people belong have been the worst hit by the oil crisis and its aftermath. They have poor natural resources, negligible foreign exchange reserves, and now they are damaged not only directly by the increase in the prices of their oil and fertilisers, but by the imported inflation set off by the rise in oil prices. On top of all that, the world prices of many of their commodities have fallen.

This is not the best time to remind the developed world of its duty to the less fortunate. On the heels of a savage inflation, the West has suffered its worst recession since the Great Depression of the thirties, with levels of unemployment which had been considered unthinkable since the adoption of Keynesian economic policies after the war. But it is well, throughout the tit-for-tat debate in which industrial and developing countries indulge, to remember how comparatively well off the average citizen of a developed country is.

Compared with the poorest of his fellow human beings, his intake of calories is 40 per cent greater, his literacy rate four times higher, the mortality rate of his children 90 per cent lower, and his own life expectancy 50 per cent greater. With those figures in mind, aid ought not to be regarded as an optional extra to be afforded when the rich world is feeling affluent, and abandoned when we are having a harder time.

What makes it more difficult, however, to persuade ordinary people, and therefore decision takers, in the West that they must do more to help the Third World is their doubts about the internal structures of those societies. It is no service to the cause of mutual understanding to dodge this issue, or pretend it does not exist, for that simply encourages the dialogue of the deaf which too often goes on between the two worlds.

The developing countries tend to lecture the West on the need for co-operation on trade, aid and a new international division of labour, but they are quite nationalistic in asserting their own right to absolute sovereignty in their own affairs. This, again, discourages even constructive criticism from outside. The New International Economic Order is a nationalistic rather than a socialist document. Whether its influence is great or not remains to be seen. New rules of the international game are needed all right, but the New International Economic Order, as the ILO commented, in a masterpiece of understatement, 'is not yet defined with precision, nor accepted without reservation by all countries'. Or as one official remarked, with less blandness: 'The sooner we separate the commonsense from the bullshit, the sooner we'll make progress.'

What the ILO has been doing, both in the World Employment Programme, which has been going on since 1969, and in preparation for its conference, is to inject a social content into this New Order. That is where the trade-off, mentioned in the previous chapter, comes in. Can enlightened statesmen in the West use the non-aligned governments' wish for a transformation of the world's economic system as a lever to open the hierarchical societies of the poorer countries themselves? Can they force the complementary reform in those countries?

It will be difficult to find the words. The West has a guilt complex about former colonies, and it has traditionally been careful about the advice it gives and the way in which it is given. Gunnar Myrdal, whose *Asian Drama* remains one of the great commentaries on the Third World, has remarked on our extreme fastidiousness, for example, in the euphemistic terminology which has converted 'under developed' countries into 'developing' ones. With greater temerity, he has also commented on the reluctance of international scholars to analyse corruption, even though it is a common subject of conversation in many developing countries and is mentioned often in speeches and in newspapers.

Corruption is important both because of its corrosive effect in the country where it occurs, and because of the dampener it puts on the sympathies of the world. Indeed, Myrdal gives a powerful impression of a disease which sours relations on both sides, with intellectuals in the developing country blaming Western businessmen for corrupting its politicians and officials — what Nasser called a 'new imperialism' — and the businessmen huffily finding it impossible to operate without paying to middlemen what amounts to a scale fee of corruption, a percentage of the value of the contract sought, which may or may not be distributed to higher officials.

It would be wrong to leave the impression that most of the criticism of Third World corruption comes from the West. It is freely discussed, and abhorred, by many people in developing countries who know what is going on. An Indian government report, for example, analyses 'speed money', which is paid not for the purpose of getting anything improper done, but simply to speed a file through the prolonged bureaucratic process. The difficulty, of course, is that officials are tempted to slow files down even more, in order to create a reason for being bribed. The deadening effect on an already inefficient system may be imagined. In Asia, bribes are said to be most common in public works and government purchasing departments, and for officials who control import and export licences, collect customs duties and taxes, and manage the railways.

The stories from Latin American countries are even more lurid. I once heard from separate and impeccable sources of an airline official on an inaugural flight from Europe who opened his suitcase to show that it was packed with dollar bills. He proposed to distribute these to officials at the South American airport to ensure that his flights were enabled to operate efficiently. He made a serious misjudgement, however, when during his speech at the airport, the freight hold of his plane was opened, revealing a Rolls Royce, which he presented to the local minister of transport. It was not that the minister resented this somewhat ostentatious public gift — on the contrary. But after the ceremony two officials drew the airline chief to one side, murmured sadly that the minister was to lose his job that weekend, and introduced his successor. A second Rolls was duly flown out.

It is worth mentioning corruption here because for many Westerners it seems like the tip of an iceberg of inequality in the Third World. They contrast the rhetoric of socialism, with which they feel themselves lambasted in international forums, with the reality of life in developing countries. They are sceptical about whether the benefits from changes in trade and aid, to which they may agree, will ever reach the poor. They believe that the ruling élite in the Third World has a total contempt for the 40 per cent of its own people living below the poverty line. Westerners who would be willing to make sacrifices — or perhaps, cynically, to allow others in their own countries to make sacrifices — in order to help impoverished peasants in the small *shambas* of the Kenyan bush, are less happy at the thought that their money will find its way into the glass-and-concrete belt of Nairobi, many of whose inhabitants are much richer than most people in the donor nations.

In all this also, of course, there is a streak of hypocrisy. It is a malleable conscience that finds it intolerable to have wealth and poverty cheek-by-jowl in a developing country, yet sees nothing wrong with the great contrasts between the living standards of the Third World and the rich, white countries. Is there much difference in logic, after all, between staying in a five-star hotel in Calcutta while a beggar dies on the footpath outside and staying in a five-star hotel in London or New York while the same death takes place on the other side of the earth? No man is an island, even if geography has distanced him and his country from the worst poverty of the human race. As television brings famine into our living rooms around the world, ignorance of the facts, or carelessness of their consequences, almost becomes wilful.

The ILO is even-handed in acknowledging that, even in the period of growth since the Second World War and since many countries gained their independence, neither of these gaps has narrowed. Between rich and poor countries, it has tended to widen. Within developing countries, the great masses of people have not benefited from economic growth, and on present trends most of Africa and Asia will become less

rather than more equal by the end of the century. The fruits
of growth have gone to a minority — including the unionised
wage earners of urban manufacturing industry. These form an
aristocracy of labour when compared with the much larger
numbers of people who, either in the countryside or in the
shanty towns round large cities, scrape a living which has the
barest connection with the cash economy.

It is difficult to grasp the scale of the poverty and
inequality we are talking about. For hundreds of millions of
people, life is abject, unemployment having reached crisis
levels, with underemployment and inadequate incomes even
more serious. To take India, the largest of the poorest: it has
been said that a population of 600 people contains within it a
facsimile of the population of France — something less than
60 million people, with resources ranging from those of a
Parisian millionaire to those of a Breton peasant. But beneath
that level, beneath the living standard of the peasant in
Brittany, are the vast masses of the Indian people. A German
economist, lecturing in Bremen, brought the scale of the
employment problem home to his audience in an equally
graphic way. Bremen had a population of 600,000, he said.
About 6,000 new people came on to the Indian labour
market each day. Therefore, the task in India was to create
additional jobs for the entire population of Bremen every
hundred days.

It is to face problems of this magnitude that a series of
world conferences has been held during the past few
years — on population, food, industrialisation, environmental
problems, and the New International Economic Order. The
World Employment Programme and the ILO's conference on
the same subject in the summer of 1976 lie within the same
tradition. The ultimate objective is no less than the elimination of mass poverty and unemployment. The ILO felt that
the pivotal role of employment was not recognised in the
UN's Second Development Decade, which covered the
seventies. It is trying to ensure that the eighties will be
different. In its vast research effort, which has taken
employment missions and individual researchers to many
countries, and larger Comprehensive Employment Missions to
seven, the ILO has set out to fill the gaps in knowledge. The

objectives of the World Employment Conference include the propagation of the new ideas which have been pulled together from hundreds of different pieces of research.

The theme is now clear: it is not a question of national policies *or* international action. Both are needed. The ILO's seven missions are proposing for each country comprehensive national strategies which would attack income disparities, correct imbalances in the educational systems, make better choices of technology, and break down the sharp divisions within developing economies between the traditional and the modern sectors. The aim would be a framework for development which would allow the mass of the people to benefit from economic growth. The ILO has no doubt that strategies which concentrate on employment are the best means of getting rid of mass poverty. A fairer incomes distribution would, in turn, create a home market, and that would generate faster growth.

But the Third World's argument that there can be no wholly national solution to a poor country's problems is freely accepted:

> Developments over the past decade [says a recent ILO document] have demonstrated time and again how even the minor ripples in the industrialised centre of the international system grow into tidal movements when they reach the developing economies, and convulse them in a manner which makes internal adjustments of little avail. More recently, the energy crisis, global inflation, monetary instability and food shortages have strikingly demonstrated the interdependence of different parts of the world economy and the extreme vulnerability of the poorer developing countries to major changes in the international economic system.

Faced with a problem of such acknowledged scale, the current world performance on aid is abysmal. Most countries are little more than halfway towards the targets set for them in 1970. Studies by the World Bank have shown that movement of prices, volume of trade, inflation and other trends which affect aid have slowed economic progress in nearly all the developing during the past few years. In some, as Mr William Clark, a vice-president of the Bank says, this has 'created an atmosphere of defeat, despair and retreat'.

Mr Clark analyses the reasons with the tact of an international official, but realistically none the less. What is needed is a new agreement by the advanced countries of the West and of Eastern Europe, together with those OPEC countries who are experiencing or expecting large financial surpluses, to transfer resources to the poorest nations. He freely admitted that the targets set by the UN had 'not attracted the necessary political support' in most of the larger industrial countries. Among some OPEC countries the targets were scarcely relevant, because with small populations and large financial surpluses, they do not have to find their aid money from taxes. OPEC countries have begun to assume their responsibilities for aid, though one complaint is that there is a strong bias among the Arab nations in favour of other Moslem countries; Pakistan, for example, seems to be faring better than India or Bangladesh.

Yet for both psychological and deeply practical reasons, aid is not the main issue, except in the short-term. Where a new order in international relations is most needed is in trade. This does not need to rely solely on an appeal to moral responsibility or generosity in the richer countries. That is just as well, for one must accept that such appeals are now suffering under the law of diminishing returns. Trade also appeals to mutual interest. Looked at from the Third World's point of view, exports are the most important means of earning money for development, as well as immediately raising living standards through wages. The richer countries would also benefit from a more rational division of labour in the world, for their consumers would get many of their goods and services more cheaply if every kind of barrier to trade were removed.

The common good, however, is not always identical with the good of the individual. Although almost anyone, reading the case for producing textiles in India rather than a developed country, can see its economic sense, this carries little conviction to a textile worker in New England, Lancashire or Yorkshire who is going to lose his job. Adjustment assistance by governments is much talked about, but its past record is uneven, to say the least. Many in Lancashire, for example, may still remember the cancellation of a military aircraft contract there in the mid-sixties. The great government theory was that this would release valuable skilled engineers for the kind of more productive work that would help to put the country on its feet. Months later many of the skilled men had become door-to-door salesmen or clerks, or had suffered long periods of unemployment.

Working people in industrial countries have a scepticism about the economic belief that immutable laws solve such problems of adjustment. In the long run they do, but in the long run we are all dead. Even the fact that the Yorkshire textile worker may have brown skin and have been born in India or Pakistan does not help. Economists would argue, with justice, that he proves their case. Why suffer the appalling personal and social upheavals of these great migrations if by a more rational division of production around the world we can enable people to earn a decent living near where they were born and presumably would prefer to live?

The answer of millions of workers, white, brown, black or yellow, is similar: that it won't happen quickly enough, that he would starve if he waited for economists, international experts, civil servants or governments to look after him. So he migrates from the Third World or he stays put in his developed country; he finds a job or he sticks to his job; he encourages his union in his new country or his old country to support the agitation for trade protection. And if he has come from the Third World, he knows that such protection may hurt his old neighbours, but it will preserve his own job and those of his new neighbours.

It is sad that the world is entering the crucial discussions of the next few years in the toils of a recession. Negotiations in GATT, in the United Nations Conference on Trade and Development (UNCTAD), and in the ILO's World Employment Conference would have had a much greater chance of success if they had been discussing ways to distribute prosperity more fairly. A moving car is easy to steer, but a static car's steering wheel is much harder to haul around.

Even before the seriousness of the recession was realised, Henry Kissinger, the United States Secretary of State, argued that 'economic expansion in the industrial world and economic co-operation with the less-developed countries go hand in hand.' He maintained that an expanding world economy is essential for development, because it stimulates trade, investment and technology; supports bilateral and multilateral aid programmes; assures growing markets for the raw materials, manufactures and agricultural products of the developing countries; provides the best framework for agreement on the divisive issues of food, energy, raw materials, trade and investment.

Leaders of the Third World would be wise to study this speech, delivered in Paris in May 1975, if only to let them see through Kissinger's eyes the oil crisis, its effects on the West, and the implications for world co-operation. To him the central test of statesmanship is the orderly reconciliation of conflicting interests and the prevention of a slide into political and economic warfare. Then he gives a widespread Western view of OPEC's actions: 'Misused economic power, as the past two years have borne stark witness, can reverse the trend of worldwide growth and retard progress for everyone. An international system will be stable only so long as its economic benefits are widely shared and its arrangements perceived as just.'

Most Third World politicians would say "amen" to his last sentence, but they ought also to heed his warning that confrontation and co-operation are bad bed-fellows. He warned against 'international meetings that exhaust themselves in self-indulgent rhetoric or self-righteous propaganda'. As for 'bloc pressure tactics', Kissinger suggested, in a passage which may cause resentment but was nevertheless true, that in trials of strength it is not the advanced countries who pay the highest price but 'the poorest and most disadvantaged, those in whose name and for whose benefits these tactics are purportedly used'.

Perhaps the most enlightening passage was that about the dilemma of the West's democracy:

Economic stagnation breeds political instability. For the

nations of the industrialised world, the economic crisis has
posed a threat to much more than our national income. It
has threatened the stability of our institutions and the
fabric of our co-operation on the range of political and
security problems. Governments cannot act with assurance
while their economies stagnate and they confront increasing domestic and international pressures over the
distribution of economic benefit. In such conditions, the
ability to act with purpose, to address either our national
or international problems, will falter. If we are to
contribute to world security and prosperity, the industrialised nations must be economically strong and politically cohesive.

To some people I met in my journey round the world, that
paragraph will be read as a squeal of pain from the privileged
of the earth, evoking less sympathy than wry amusement at
the plight of those who have had life too easy for too long.
Yet no one who has observed with dismay the growth of
introspection in the West as the recession deepens can ignore
the seriousness of those words for the Third World, as for us
all. At a time when we need a Marshall Plan on a global scale,
the strongest nations have become increasingly preoccupied
with their own balance of payments, their own inflation,
their own unemployment. Again, it is as natural and human
as the Third World's anger and despair at the suffering of its
own people. But the inwardness it produces is ultimately
self-defeating and dangerous to us all. The world desperately
needs realistic generosity from the West, but it will scarcely
come from politicians with their backs to the wall.

The danger is that we will all settle into a corrosive
squabble about the distribution of diminishing wealth.
Already in the West, there are signs that the Keynesian vision
is fading. The leading members of the Organisation for
Economic Co-operation and Development (OECD), the
keepers of the Ark of the Covenant for the Marshall Plan
which revived Europe at the end of the war, are gently
quarrelling among themselves. How can they lead the world
out of recession without again stoking up the disastrous
inflation of the years since the oil crisis? The tendency, even

within that group, is to put national self-interest before the good of other countries. The rational fact that not every country can simultaneously enjoy a balance of payments surplus is lost in the pursuit of national economic health in a sick world.

There is every chance that this myopia will be matched and surpassed on a world scale. The Third World's demands for a greater share of earth's wealth is both understandable and just in the light of the present growth inequalities. Yet its rhetoric, which pays only lip service to co-operation with the West, may be self-defeating, particularly as it ignores two vital elements. The first, already dealt with, is Western irritation at the failure to tackle inequity within Third World countries. The second is more complex.

Although the richer nations, and particularly their working people, feel that they have run into a period of extreme hardship, and although they fear that the recession, like that of the thirties, may be prolonged, their position looks quite different when viewed from the Third World. The developed countries are incredibly rich when looked at from India, Tanzania, Indonesia or Mexico. Even their poor are rich. So will it be such a tragedy if their living standards fall a bit?

That question is very natural, coming from Third World politicians and officials, who see many of their own countrymen in much more extreme want, who know they have little chance of achieving anything like a tolerable living standard for the masses of their people, and who desperately need the help which the West seems willing to supply only in the most cheese-paring way.

But this attitude misses one essential fact that Kissinger hinted at: the Western countries from whom concessions are needed are democracies. Their governments depend on the votes of even the least rich and powerful of their people. The temptation for the Third World to bully its way to a better share of the world's wealth is great. But it probably will not succeed.

Neither, however, can the West afford to sit on a defensive rampart, its hand on its musket. Both sides will lose, as they have already lost, by trials of strength like that set off by OPEC in the autumn of 1973. Agreement between such disparate countries with such apparently conflicting interests will be difficult. Yet this is still the best, probably the only way. The choice is between mutual help and mutual destruction. This book is about mutual help.

3 Kenya: a Society in the Balance

It isn't easy to engineer a society. This one happens to be a capitalist success story. — American economist in Kenya

Kenya has no ideology. The system is the same as in 1960, only rich blacks have replaced the rich whites. The African bourgeoisie is an élite also. Kenya will have to go Left. I would rather bet on Tanzania than Kenya. — Scandinavian economist

There is slightly more freedom in Kenya than in Tanzania. They still say what they like, rather than mouthing government slogans. And there is more dynamism in the economy. — Kenyan economist.

The sharply contrasting views in the epigraphs above were answered by a Kenyan politician:

Of course we fear that the ruling class and the middle class will take too much. Corruption is universal. But remember that the people accused of pocketing the biggest share have also been responsible for the principal increases in production. In a country like this you've got to put the emphasis on production. We make too much fuss about the small number of people who control the 'kick' in Kenya. In any society the group which controls things is small.

Whenever work and poverty are discussed in Kenya, the comparison with Tanzania arises inevitably. Like the comparison between India and China, this lies at the heart of one of the fundamental arguments over Third World development. It is the contrast between the steel and concrete skyscrapers of Nairobi and the Tanzanian Ujamaa co-operative village, between modified capitalism and African socialism. Like all such arguments, the comparison provides a convincing answer only for those who needed no convincing in the first place, for those with a firm ideological commitment to either private enterprise or socialism. I preferred the judicial comment of a member of the Kenyan government, who said that, although he personally preferred the Kenyan model of development, it would probably not be possible for another generation to say which suited Africa better.

Kenya, like most other countries, is a prisoner of its history. Colonial society was based on the huge British farms. The other races had their allotted roles: the Asians as tradesmen and shopkeepers, the Africans as unskilled labourers. Since the Africans were forbidden to grow cash crops on their smallholdings (shambas), they had to work on European farms and plantations if they were to penetrate the cash economy at all. But the colonial government kept rural wages low and used higher wages to attract workers to the cities.

With growing prosperity in the boom years after the Second World War, more and more Africans were drawn into Nairobi and Mombasa to provide the goods and services demanded by the relatively affluent Europeans. This produced a dual society, with reasonably well paid jobs for the better educated in the towns and abject poverty in the countryside. It has not changed much today. What strikes the visitor from an industrial country as the outstanding difference in a society like Kenya is the status of the wage earners in large-scale industry. They are part of a privileged class, and when the issue of redistributing incomes is raised, the conservative faction is always likely to include trade unions, whose members stand to lose.

Because of the Mau Mau emergency in the fifties, the colonial administration tried to modify the dual system before independence, but it was too late; a society divided between a comparatively small urban élite and a large, impoverished and mostly rural population had been established. Independence has perpetuated that division. A society which was organised for the benefit of European farmers, businessmen and officials, with their high incomes, produced a pattern of consumption which was not easily changed.

Independence has merely given educated Africans the chance to aspire to the life-styles of their former colonial masters. It sometimes seems the only change is in the colour of the faces.

A new élite, enjoying the legitimacy which independence has conferred on them, have a vested interest in perpetuating the dual society. This has important implications for the educational system, for a high income and a middle-class way of life depend on obtaining the kind of education which leads to a white-collar job. For the individual, it makes sense. But is it the best way to develop the Kenyan economy, or to help the many millions of Kenyans who cannot hope to join what the planners call the formal sector? The scale of rural poverty and the growing body of people drawn to the cities in the vain search for a job make an explosive political mixture.

Because of this, an atmosphere of gathering crisis now hangs over Kenya. It was sharpened during 1975 by the unexplained murder of J.M. Kariuki, an MP who had been critical of the government. To many Kenyans the crisis seems unfair, for their independence had until recently looked like one of the success stories of Africa. Partly this was due to the political stability which Jomo Kenyatta has managed — up to the time of writing — to give to the country; partly to the enterprising nature of the dominant tribe, the Kikuyu.

Since independence in 1963, Kenya has enjoyed one of the highest growth rates in the developing world, a consistent 7 or 8 per cent. Nairobi has become the most dynamic city in black Africa. All seemed to be going well — except that the prosperous were getting more prosperous, and the poor, both those in the countryside and the slum dwellers of Nairobi, were sinking further into their poverty. In the cities a quarter of the people do not earn enough to live on, and in the country as many as two out of five are in the same position. Between a quarter and a half of Kenya's children suffer some malnutrition.

Even before the world inflation of the early seventies, the country was heading for trouble, what the World Bank called 'unmanageable balance of payments problems'. But the oil inflation turned a problem into a crisis. Although the prices of Kenya's exports rose, they could not keep pace with the cost of imports. Severe domestic inflation, which 'Kenya had previously escaped, was added to balance of payments problems. No one now expects the terms of trade to turn back in Kenya's favour, and one estimate is that they will deteriorate by as much as 24 per cent between 1973 and 1978.

Fortunately, some new ideas for dealing with the crisis were to hand. An ILO comprehensive employment mission had visited Kenya in 1972. The strategy it proposed was 'redistribution of the fruits of growth'. Its policies were designed to diminish the sharp imbalances in Kenyan society through a complete restructuring of the economy. It was critical of the way in which Kenya had used its independence, and blamed unemployment and underemployment on failure to introduce radical changes aimed at greater income distribution and productive work for all. The report estimated the average unemployment rate in the towns at 15 per cent, but it regarded the working poor, in the towns and in the country, as an even greater problem.

It is not a self-righting problem. Nine out of ten Kenyans still live in the country. With one of the fastest population growth rates in the world — 3½ per cent each year — the country cannot provide enough jobs by expanding modern industry, on which so much of the government's past efforts have concentrated. By the year 2000 Kenya could have between 30 and 40 million people, instead of the present 12 million.

Faced with a problem of this magnitude, the ILO mission urged that a large part of the solution must lie in the countryside. It advocated much more distribution of land, so that agriculture can be both more land- and labour-intensive — in other words, so that it can produce more, thus saving money on imports, and employ more people.

Land reform is essential to all progress in Kenya. Most of the large European farms have been taken over in the years since independence, but there is much controversy about the way in which this land has been distributed. Estimates vary about how much of it has gone to the landless poor. One observer told me that perhaps 40 per cent was given to smallholders, while 60 per cent went to large African landholders. Even the government's own sessional paper concedes that in the first land distribution after independence nearly half of the European land taken over was kept in estates of more than 800 acres. There has been shameless grabbing of land by politicians, civil servants, and others with political clout. This is the most extreme symbol of the greed of the Kenyan élite, a simple-minded determination among those who rule a new country to carry on where the Europeans they drove out had left off.

One international expert said with distaste: 'This is still a poor country, yet 3 per cent of its people live in abundance. The corruption is blatant. They don't even bother to conceal the fact that everything is up for grabs.'

Supporters of the regime argue that large farms are more efficient. This is sometimes true; it is said particularly of some of the wheat farms which are still in white hands. But it is also true that in many areas of the country land is shamefully underused, and that it could be much more intensively cultivated if it were handed over to poor people who have no land of their own.

The absence so far of really radical land reform has created a crisis in many families. With large numbers of children and small holdings, the number of times that the family plot can be divided among the sons is limited. Some young peasants decide that they must get out. Here history enters the picture again, for the poverty at home and the high wages in the city have produced in many poor Kenyan peasants an extreme reverence for education as a passport to a good standard of living. This introduces to our story a group we will meet again in Sri Lanka and elsewhere — the educated unemployed.

A labour exchange official at Nyeri, an hour's drive from Nairobi in luxuriant farming and tourist country, shook his head sadly as he talked about his country's youth. At times he sounded like an echo of rather conservative observers in Bournemouth or Halifax:

> We seem to have educated more people than we've got jobs for. The young school-leavers are selective. They won't go back to the shambas to work. They think there's

no future in the country, and they want to work and live
in town. They want white-collar jobs, in offices or shops.
If you ask them to take a job where they'd have to sweat,
they think you're a colonialist

He made it clear, however, that the youngsters he dealt
with preferred even a labouring job in town — there is a new
textile factory at Nanyuki, which is nearby — to work on
their fathers' farms. But the search for work in town is often
a long one. The ILO report records the case of Peter, a man
of twenty-three, who has been in Nairobi for four years,
seeking a job as a clerk. With seven years' schooling and a
year at a private business college, he has made ends meet in
Nairobi by living with relatives and contributing what he can
to the upkeep of their household — he occasionally folds
advertisements for a newspaper, helps his uncle in a small
shop, or buys and sells old newspapers at a small profit.
Peter's father and brother could use his help on their shamba,
but he says: 'Only illiterates work in the shambas. I had
better get a job instead, or they will treat me as an illiterate.'

Foreign experts have warned Kenya that if it wishes to
avoid the frustration that this statement conjures up, and the
dangerous political situation the frustration could create,
there ought to be a change in the pattern of remuneration, so
that people in the rural areas can earn a decent living and will
not be tempted to the cities. Although, during the period of
fast growth, the modern sector of Kenya's economy has
produced more jobs, the effect of this is to persuade still
more young men to work for still more paper qualifications,
in the hope of getting better paid work. It is a sad story of
rising but abortive expectations. Education that contains no
training for the kind of work likely to be available causes
great anguish.

The ILO report summarises it like this:

Those who succeed within the school system obtain the
certificates and the good jobs — or did at first. But as
education expanded fast, among a population itself fast
expanding, thousands of young Kenyans, with their
parents and other supporters, are beginning to find their

certificates almost worthless, at least for obtaining jobs. First it was the primary school leavers, then the Form 2 leavers, now those with school certificates, soon those with university arts degrees. This is the background to frustration among school leavers and their families.

The ILO investigators rejected the belief that the 'informal urban sector', in which many of those who drift to the city find themselves scraping a living, consisted of 'fictional, marginal, parasitical or illegal activities — those of the beggar, the shoeshine boy, the thief, the prostitute'. In fact, many of them work, or wait around in the hope of getting work, for enormously long hours, often without much to show for their efforts. The married men send home what money they can to their families in the country, but often the wife finds herself struggling alone to keep the shamba going, without much support coming back from the city.

A visitor to Nairobi quickly discovers that the skills of this informal sector are much more elaborate than its critics realise. Not far from the city centre, though in one of the slummier districts, are to be found panel beaters who will repair accident damage to your car at a fraction of the price charged by ordinary garages. The work is carried out in the street, though sometimes with quite elaborate equipment and tools brought each day from the workman's home. The more cynical observer, to the distress of the idealists, warns you that it's still wise to leave someone guarding the car while the work is being done; otherwise the headlamps may disappear.

The ILO men praised the enterprise of such informal businessmen, and said they had no alternative but to make a living by catering, as tailors, masons, carpenters, or café owners, for the wants of their fellow citizens — principally those, like themselves, who cannot push their way into the more lucrative employment of the formal sector. One Kenyan sociologist summed up the contrast between the informal and the modern parts of the economy like this: 'It's Mama Njeri's kitchen versus the Nairobi Hilton.' In one, the ordinary African can get a cheap meal, cooked by his own kind; in the other a middle-class bourgeoisie, African as well as expatriate, enjoys the more lavish standards of international cuisine and life-style.

The authorities had long taken a dim view of the informal urban sector, and they find it hard to break the habit. Research workers collecting data in the Nairobi slums have often found themselves only a short jump ahead of the city council's bulldozers. The tradition of demolishing everything that was not *comme il faut* goes back to the earlier colonial period, when the British were still trying to keep Nairobi an all-white city. Since independence the council has been just as ruthless. Slums are often cleared without any rehousing scheme being ready. Even when it is, the deeply ingrained instincts of the Kikuyu for profit sometimes thwart the planners. When low-cost housing was provided for some slum dwellers a year or two ago, they decided that it was not cheap enough, so they moved back to their shanties and promptly let their new homes to other unfortunate people — at a profit. Official policies designed to guard against fire, health and other dangers are not working. Near one new housing estate, the land is empty during the day, but at night hundreds of families build dwellings of stick frames covered by cardboard or cloth. As the sun rises, they fold up their tents and steal away.

Many people think the Nairobi council is trying to enforce impossibly high health standards for an African city. Even when there is a possibility of dealing satisfactorily with health hazards, the council's behaviour often seems bureaucratic and eccentric. Recently a foreign firm offered to replace the somewhat unhygienic tea bars to be seen in the poorer areas with a chain of low-cost kiosks. These were to be let to the original tenants. But the council gave the new kiosks to the highest bidders.

Generally, the licensing system appears extremely illiberal. It preserves monopoly, rather than helping the small man to get started. At times there has been extensive trading in licences, with widespread corruption. After recent criticism, the government has promised to reform the system. But what is really needed is a transformation of the government's own attitude towards its urban poor. Because the interests of Kenya's privileged groups lie in manufacturing or large-scale agriculture, they have been slow to realise that the small family businesses of the Nairobi slums may contain one of the best hopes for growth in the future.

As one Nairobi academic put it to me, 'money runs faster in that kind of life.' Or as the economists prefer to say, there are greater possibilities of capital accumulation than in large-scale industry which, with present balance of payments difficulties, is going to find imported machinery and raw materials more and more difficult to obtain. The government is now promising to give more contracts and to encourage sub-contracting to the small men. It is a policy which has worked well for many years in Calcutta, and it is surprising that it has taken so long for Kenya to follow suit. After all, between a quarter and a third of people who work in towns are not engaged in modern industry or services. It is a large proportion of your population to forget.

In the countryside, land reform is only one of the necessary changes. The ILO and other reports have also underlined the need for technology appropriate to a developing country. One of the successes of the report, here as in other countries, has been its impact on road building methods. I went with an enthusiastic Norwegian civil engineer, Eilif Eide, to see the scheme he has helped to create near Nyeri. At first, there was understandable resistance in Kenya to labour-intensive methods of road building. Everywhere in the Third World, there is a fear that Europeans will continue to regard them as coolie labour. Under colonial rule in Kenya, not only convicts, but conscripted African labour was employed on the roads. In recent years, mechanised methods have been used, and a report to the World Bank by a consulting engineer in 1968 appears to have suggested that these were much more economical. Eide believes he has now proved that this is not so. He says that the adverse report estimated that it was one-third cheaper to use all-mechanised rather than all-labour methods. But he argues that this is not the equation, for you can reduce costs by a further 10 per cent by using the appropriate mixture of the two methods. If this system is to work, however, more of the rich countries will have to be willing to give their aid money for paying local wages, rather than insist that it be used for importing their own bulldozers and other heavy building equipment.

Watching the Nyeri project, one sees how the mixed method works. A road is being constructed to serve a scattering of shambas. At present their produce is carried to market on the backs of the women. When it was decided to build a road, the local engineer, a Dutchman, Jan de Veen, approached the chief, who is paid by the government to be a channel between the administration and his people. He called a baraza, or tribal meeting, and introduced 'the Great Road Man'. De Veen then explained the benefits the community would get from the road, but pointed out that those with shambas on either side of the existing track would have to give up small portions of their land for bridges etc. Precious though land is to the Kenyan peasant, they agreed. The thought of the pick-up truck running past their farms to collect produce for market was enough.

He also explained that the second benefit was that it would provide paid work for many of the men folk. This would be at minimum rates — a little over 5 Kenyan shillings (less than a dollar) a day. It would be casual employment, with no pay for sickness or days off. People are so keen to get work in this area that some are willing to walk up to 10 kilometres a day to the job. There are usually more volunteers than are needed, and selection is by lottery. Supervision has to be quite strict, for there is no tradition of working for an employer among people in the area. In some projects a system of task work is used: the men can go home as soon as they have finished their allotted task.

Eide likes to explain that he is not so ideological about labour-intensive methods that he wants to take the African peasant back to the days of moving earth by head basket. 'Appropriate' is the word for his kind of technology. The day I was there, the gang was filling in a section of the proposed route which ran through low-lying, marshy land, the drainage complicated by a nearby railway line and by dams which had been built to irrigate adjoining shambas. The soil was being moved about 50 metres by wheelbarrow. This allows each man to move between 2.5 and 3 cubic metres a day. Eide reckons it is economical to use wheelbarrows up to at least 75 metres. For greater distances, a tractor and trailer would be used. One of the labourers I talked with said that he had been at school until he was twenty, and had worked for a year since that on his father's shamba. But the produce and the income from the farm was not really enough to support the family, so when the road building began the father had told him to get a job there. This was both because they wanted the road to get their maize and tomatoes to market more easily, and because they needed the wage money. The young man complained that the pay was too low, with prices rising as they were, but like many others he seemed to think that any job was better than none.

The government is also establishing, in accordance with the ILO Mission's ideas, a chain of rural industry development centres. One which I visited specialised in woodwork and metalwork. Local men were brought in to be trained, and were allowed to use the machinery and equipment for jobs for their own outside customers. They were charged a small rent for the machinery and for materials used, but the remainder of the price they received for their tables, cupboards or metal water containers was profit. The objective is to establish rural skills and crafts which will keep people in the country and stop still more hurrying off for the higher wages in Nairobi.

But has the main thrust of government policy been changed by the growing storm of criticism at home and abroad? Advice from the ILO, the World Bank and other bodies has had some impact. The Minister of Finance, Mr Kibaki, had a meeting with the international agencies in Paris in the spring of 1974, and there was a marked change in policy after that. Tax and other incentives have been used to encourage labour-intensive industries using local raw materials; import duties on industrial raw materials have been raised; tax allowances which produced new industries in Nairobi and Mombasa have been withdrawn, to encourage more investors to look at the smaller towns; and higher taxes are being levied on luxury goods.

Public spending is also being devoted more to projects which benefit the poor — minor dirt roads rather than trunk roads, water supplies rather than government buildings. The need for this is not difficult to see: as you drive along the well built major roads, women are struggling through the hot countryside, the water for their families carried in old petrol drums balanced on their heads.

But the government seems half-hearted on the two principal themes of the ILO report, land reform and income distribution. Lip service is paid to the need for distributing land, but it is difficult to avoid the conclusion that there are too many vested interests within the régime and among its friends to allow anything radical to happen. Specifically, the proposal for a ceiling on the size of holdings looked far too much for the Establishment to swallow.

As for income distribution, the government shied away from the more radical measures proposed by the ILO, including a total freeze for five years on the incomes of those earning about $2000 or more. The reasons are not hard to see. Already the better off workers in the towns are feeling the pinch from the world recession and inflation and its effects in Kenya. But most of the political influence resides with just such groups, and they, as well as the business community and the large landowners, stand to lose if there is extensive redistribution of wealth in favour of the three-quarters of the households which live on less than $300 a year.

These less well off people, mostly smallholders or the urban working poor, often lack access to education, training, health facilities, water and credit. The ILO's plan, drawn up before the recession, hoped that if Kenya could continue growth and if the richest one-tenth of her people would accept a freeze on their incomes, the poorest families might double their standards of living by the mid-eighties. These now look like two very large 'ifs'.

Since much of this chapter has reported criticism of the Kenya government's attitudes, it is fair also to report that there is a strong body of thought in Nairobi, including some foreign observers and independent African academics, which has held that the ILO and other international proposals are unrealistic. What follows is a compendium of their criticisms:

The ILO proposals were conceptually prejudiced. The mission came with their minds made up about the effects of a capitalist economy. Despite the glaring inequalities,

Kenyan society is dynamic. There is development every-where — schools, hospitals, water supplies and so on. Tanzania, by contrast, has to rely on foreign aid even to feed its people.

Outside advice, in this as in other countries, takes too little notice of local realities. Investigators arrive *parti pris*. For example, in considering Kenya you have to remember that the Kikuyu, deprived under colonialism of the chance to trade, took to private enterprise like ducks to water. In trying to alter the social attitudes of Kenyan society, the ILO is taking on the world. Where is Kenyatta expected to start? The people who support his government, who must sustain any government in Kenya at present, are willing enough to help the deprived sections of society. But not at their own expense.

One manager argued that a limitation on the incomes of the better off in order to help the poor was politically impossible, because both unions and managers opposed it. An industrialist argued more fundamentally against a change of direction. It was wrong, he said, to believe that the benefits of industrialisation did not filter down at present to poor people. The extended family system in Africa ensured that they did. Kenya might not have a social security system like a Western country, but each reasonably affluent man had 'a plethora of hangers-on, who come in droves, looking for a hand-out for a taxi'. (The sweep of his rhetoric prevented my asking whether the suppliants wanted only the fare to hire a taxi home to the slums, or whether they would require enough money to buy one and set up in trade.)

His contrast, inevitably, was with Tanzania. The reason that Kenya was more advanced than Tanzania was that while Tanzania had solved its grossest imbalances of wealth, it had not effectively discovered how to create efficient production. There was an extremely lackadaisical approach. This was because there was no incentive to work. In any society, the middle class was the group which planned and initiated. In Tanzania, that was the most frustrated group. People worked at the pace of the slowest.

'Political rhetoric is not enough,' he declared, warming to

his theme. 'I don't just want to be praised as a good socialist worker. I want some incentive for myself.'

In support of this view, a politician argued that more and more people in Kenya, under the existing system, were getting a toe into the cash economy. Tea, coffee, cotton, pyrethrum and other crops are now produced by small-holders. Fishermen on the coast are being helped to reach the markets with their catches. Milk produced on the shambas is being sold to the dairies.

The ups and downs of change are illustrated by two of these products. Pyrethrum has had its value boosted by the reaction against DDT and the need for other forms of insect control. This is a useful addition to farm income. But although the introduction of co-operative dairy methods has also increased cash incomes from milk, this has not always had a good effect on family diets: the milk is now sometimes disposed of commercially, rather than being given to the children. Instead, they are offered fizzy orange drinks whose nutritional value is nil.

With all its ups and downs, Kenya is undoubtedly making progress. The charge of its critics is that progress is too slow, and that the menace of rising population and growing social discontent will engulf the country if the government does not take drastic action to produce a more equitable society quickly. Perhaps the fairest defence to that was put by a government minister who conceded that they would have to go further on land reform, perhaps even to a ceiling on estates. But he said that it must be remembered that Kenya's independence struggle had been about land as well as freedom, and you had to be extremely careful about how you proceeded. The underlying issue between the Kenyan and Tanzanian methods was this: Would reliance on redistribution not only of land, but of wealth generally, delay the development that Kenya desperately needs? The ILO's answer to that question, in Kenya as elsewhere, is no. That is the issue now being thrashed out around the Third World.

4 Sri Lanka:
Educated but Jobless

In the cloisters around the swimming pool of my hotel in Colombo hung some framed and illustrated poems from one of those slim Victorian volumes produced by Vereker M. Hamilton and Stewart M. Fasson, *Scenes in Ceylon* (1879–80). Theirs was the colonial world of a century ago, with the natives waiting for the four o'clock hooter that allowed them to stop work, assisting the British in their deer driving or elephant hunting, watching admiringly while the gentry played polo, or driving their masters and mistresses on the Galle Face Mall, beside the Indian Ocean, among a throng which must have looked like Bath transported to the East.

In a verse of inspired banality, Hamilton and Fasson — were they subalterns or Colonial Office chaps? — describe this scene of the British Empire at its zenith:

> It seems a rule of nature's school
> That every land can boast of
> Some drive or mall where beau and belle
> Their charms can make the most of.

That lost world is oddly relevant to the modern enigma of Sri Lanka. It remains the highly traditional society that pre-independence Ceylon also was, yet it has a strong and long-standing Marxist tradition, and until recently its coalition government contained members of the only ruling Trotskyist party in the world, working in more or less harmonious accord with the social democrats of Mrs Bandaranike's Sri Lanka Freedom Party.

Ceylon has had an enviably stable political democracy

since independence in 1947, with governments changing regularly through the ballot box rather than the coup. Yet although it is a politically conscious Third World society, it seems to have taken all its values from the British, and to have retained them long after they have been abandoned by their creators. Most significantly, this failure to break cleanly with the colonial past dominates the educational and career structure, where many Ceylonese are still striving for the jobs, social status, and life-style that they must have envied among the British all those years ago.

As a result, Ceylon represents one of the worst cases of educated unemployment in the Third World — though its present difficulties have been described as 'a horoscope of Asia's future'. When members of an ILO mission were in Colombo in 1971, looking for ways in which this and other employment problems could be tackled, they had vivid, personal confirmation of how serious its effects could be: Ceylon's first insurrection, a rising led by young educated people who could not get jobs, caused them to be confined to their hotel by a curfew for several days.

Where did Ceylon go wrong? The inheritance at independence was in some ways enviable, but difficult all the same. In 130 years the British had created an elaborate road and railway system which made even the mountainous areas accessible, built up the towns, developed the Port of Colombo, and created a modern administration and a system of courts which has largely survived. The new country also inherited its two double-edged benefits — the tea, rubber and coconut plantations, and the educational system, which is far more developed and comprehensive than that in most other developing countries.

The plantations grew up in the middle of the nineteenth century, first producing coffee, and then moving on to tea. To grow these crops for the European market, as well as to develop the rubber and coconut crops, the British owners brought almost all their labour from South India. Between 1840 and 1920, the Tamil estate workers came flooding in, sometimes at the rate of 1000 a week. By 1945 it was reckoned that there were more than 600,000 of them, more than a quarter of the Ceylon labour force, and equal to the number working in the rest of agriculture. One problem is that these people, distinguished by culture, language and often by lack of Ceylonese citizenship, are almost totally separated from the rest of the economy.

The other is that the plantations distorted the whole pattern of Ceylon's foreign trade. Their exports paid for consumer goods for the British and Ceylonese upper classes, and for the imported equipment and raw materials needed in the factories which were built during the Second World War. But the estate labourers were not growing food for themselves, and as a result Ceylon built up a tradition of importing rice and other staple foods, from which it has still not freed itself. That tradition has helped to produce a foreign exchange crisis of alarming and growing proportions.

The new country also inherited an administrative system which by the time of independence was largely Ceylonised. Its members were products of an educational system modelled on that in Britain, and geared to fill places in the civil service. Since the salaries paid to Ceylonese administrators equalled those which had been received by expatriate British, and were very high compared with normal income levels, the civil service became a much sought after career. The result is that Ceylon has entered the fourth quarter of the century with one of the most developed and expensive welfare systems in the Third World, an educational system which puts a primary school within 1½ miles of every child's home, a public service whose standards of integrity are high, and a parliamentary democracy which has survived those of many other developing countries. But it has an economy based largely on one crop, tea, whose earnings are unpredictable, and an almost psychological aversion among its people to productive work.

Emphatically, this does not mean that the Ceylonese are a lazy people. But it is scarcely going too far to say that their school system has been an educational marvel and an economic disaster. It is at last being reformed, but there is no doubt that the old, irrelevant methods have survived so long because Ceylonese society has a deep attachment to the lost world of the English settler and the Ceylonese élite who successfully emulated him. This shows itself most significantly in attitudes to education and careers, but I first grasped its strength imaginatively in quite a different context.

I was invited for a drink at the home of a minister, together with some Ceylonese friends. The only stranger in the company was the local police inspector, who had a couple of stiff whiskies and then went off to the study for some private business with our host. The Ceylonese police-man was the archetype of English police officers of the pre-war era — black hair carefully parted and sleeked down, clipped accent, a handshake of painful firmness, and Estab-lishment opinions of equal firmness. Not much had changed for him since 1947.

Too little has changed for the economy, too. As the current national plan bluntly says: 'Ceylon can no longer continue on a path where consumption and the style of living of the whole nation are geared to the aspirations and motivations of a bygone era fashioned on the needs and desires of a privileged group.'

Or as Mrs Bandaranike herself puts it:

> Our country is blessed with a fertile soil, abundant natural resources and an educated population. Yet we depend on other countries for our food and essential requirements. While land and labour remain idle, we wait for the next ship to come to harbour. We import our cloth while our factories and power-looms and hand-looms remain unused. And what is worse, we do all this on credit which future generations have to pay.

Even allowing for the rhetoric of an incoming Prime Minister who could afford to blame her predecessors, these were strong words. Dudley Seers, who led the ILO mission to Ceylon, summed up the immediate economic cause of the crisis when he said that the country had not been responsive enough to developments in the world economy, particularly the sharp deterioration in Ceylon's terms of trade. But his report also pointed to a much longer-term problem, that of the educated unemployed, who cannot get the jobs they want, who will not take manual work, and who end up pursuing the chimera of a white-collar job for years. As one cynic commented, with conscious paradox: 'Unemployment is a luxury only the better-off can afford.'

Oddly and awkwardly, from the individual's point of view, as distinct from that of society, to hold out for a job in the civil service may be right. One of the strengths of Ceylonese democracy is its reverence for individual rights. As one educational administrator commented: 'In the eyes of the masses, education was almost solely a means of "getting to the top". Always the question that was asked was "how can the chances of a child from a poor home to enter the privileged circle be improved?" The question "how can education be made to contribute to the betterment of the masses of the underprivileged?" was scarcely ever raised.' The financial rewards for those who reached the charmed circle were sufficiently better than those to be earned in the drought-threatened, arduous world of farming to make many able boys hold on for even a lowly job in the public service.

The result of this is that, against an overall unemployment rate estimated at 14 per cent when the mission was in Ceylon in 1971, the figure in the 20–4 age group was 63 per cent among those who had passed O-level examinations, and 69 for those who had passed A-levels. Yet only one in ten of those passing A-levels got to university, though the examination was wholly directed to university education; and even among those who graduated from university, unemployment at that time was probably about 30 per cent. And while many thousands of young Ceylonese waited in the hope of the white-collar job to which they felt entitled by their education, the government was having to import from India workers to carry out such tasks as hoeing, weeding or building. The ILO report called the pattern of pay in Ceylon 'perverse'. Particularly because education is free, and alllowing for the risks of unemployment, climbing the educational ladder was 'still richly rewarding for those who reach the higher rungs'.

Not only has pay for government jobs been ludicrously higher than that in productive industry or agriculture. Security was also important in a country where drought and crop failure have made agriculture in some places a precarious occupation. But patronage came into the equation also. Not the least reason why a boy with O-levels — astonishingly, the

minimum qualification for almost any kind of government
employment — is prepared to be one of the many tea-boys or
general servants in a government office is that this gives him
access to the patronage of his boss, and he may be able to say
a word for a brother or a friend who also needs a job.

The sense of obligation which is forced on the élite
extends into their private lives also. A middle-rank public
official told me that he employed three servants at home
partly because he felt they needed a job more than he needed
the money their services would cost him. Jobs are also
created where none really exists in the public service. The
loser is the taxpayer, and in a poor country where the income
taxpayers are only the richest 200,000 of a workforce of
about 4 million, it is easy to think that such behaviour does
not matter and is, in fact, a perfectly reasonable piece of
human charity. Indeed, until the economic system of Ceylon
can be transformed, perhaps it is.

But the top heavy government structure and the failure to
change attitudes to productive employment, particularly in
farming, left the country in poor shape to face the economic
storm which has encompassed it in the past ten years. The
problem is that the plantation crops, tea, rubber and
coconut, have been in the doldrums for a long time, their
prices at best stable and often falling. Add to this the massive
increase in import prices, reaching a crescendo since October
1973 — prices of oil multiplied by five, of fertiliser by four,
and of imported rice by three — and a worsening foreign
exchange crisis was inevitable.

But the problem was there long before the oil crisis.
Ceylon has been living beyond her means for many years. In
the past fifteen years the earnings from tea have been nothing
like enough to pay the import bill. As the ILO report
commented:

> Her social achievements are in refreshing contrast with
> those of many other countries, but it can be asked whether
> there has been a corresponding emphasis in public life on
> the efficiency, work, thrift, even sacrifice necessary to
> maintain and develop a welfare state. In all countries there
> is a tendency for the public to look to government for

benefits, even benefits that have not been earned, and in Ceylon this tendency seems especially strong.

Subsidised rice is an example of this tendency to lean on the state. As we have seen, this again was a product of history. Ceylon was self-supporting before the first Europeans (the Portuguese) came in the sixteenth century. The elaborate irrigation systems which they had built in the dry areas of the north and east had already been damaged by wars with the Tamils, however, and when the British in the nineteenth century introduced the plantation crops, worked by Tamil labour, the importation of rice became essential. The Singhalese peasant, of course, still produced enough rice for his own use, but the colony was too busy making money out of plantation crops to worry about self-sufficiency in food.

Yet here again we come on a Ceylonese custom which has inflicted damage. Since independence successive governments have competed in paying higher subsidies on the imported rice. Free or cheap rice is even given to peasants who sell their own crops at higher rates. Now, in a country which has been a pioneer in social welfare in the Third World — not only in education, but in health and other public services — the wish to protect the poor against high prices for basic foods is understandable.

One man in Colombo told me that he believes his fellow countrymen's tendency to look to the state as the all-provider goes back even beyond colonialism to the Singhalese kings at Kandy, who undertook a feudal responsibility for the welfare of their followers. Whatever the cause, the subsidy on imported rice has been expensive both in direct terms and in the way it has discouraged home agriculture. Yet neither the present government nor its United National Party predecessor has felt able to abolish the subsidy, though a number of courageous ministers have resigned in frustration at not being allowed to face the public with harsh economic facts.

Ceylon's population has increased rapidly. The rate is now almost 3 per cent a year, and the population has almost doubled — to more than 12 million — in the last twenty five years. A successful campaign to wipe out malaria has meant that more than a million Ceylonese who would previously have died from malaria are alive. It is a remarkable medical

achievement, but it makes the country's economic slug-
gishness dangerous. An economy heavily dependent on tea
exports was not a good base for rapid expansion of welfare
services for the growing population. What was needed was the
development of new exports and the expanded production of
rice and other necessities which are at present imported. It
has been estimated that food subsidies, notably that on rice,
cost about as much as education and health put together. As
for exports, twenty years after independence the plantation
crops still accounted for 90 per cent of the country's trade.

It would not have been easy to change this. Recently
Ceylon has lost $14 million of foreign exchange annually by
a deterioration in its terms of trade. For example, tea
production increased by half over a period of eleven years.
but it earned Ceylon less in real terms. As a result, industries
have been running well below capacity because the foreign
exchange was not available to buy raw materials. Steel,
textiles, cement, and light industries have all suffered badly.
There was a lot in what one anguished and angry official in
Colombo told me: 'If the English are upset, as they appear to
be, about conditions for workers on our tea estates, they
don't need to have a boycott or anything like that. They just
have to be willing to pay a penny a pound more for their tea.
That would make all the difference.'

When the ILO Mission was in Colombo in 1971, about
550,000 people were unemployed. Now the figure is somewhere between 700,000 and 800,000. There is a lack of
precision, because the total includes many girls, particularly
in rural areas, who may not be genuinely looking for jobs,
and an uncertain number of boys who are employed,
probably on their father's farms, but who are still aspiring to
their government white collar.

Ceylon has been drifting into its crisis for more than
twenty years. When the first left-of-centre government took
power in 1956, it increased the rice subsidy and released
more spending power to the workers. This began the damage
to the foreign exchange system, just at a time when primary
price movements were beginning to hurt. The first signs of
reform and more realistic policies seemed to date from the
food crisis which hit the rice eating countries in the

mid-sixties. The UNP, returning to office in 1965, organised a massive rice growing campaign, allowed the price of imported rice to rise, and restricted the entry of other foodstuffs. The left coalition parties were scathing about this policy during the 1970 election, and on returning to office they raised the rice subsidy again. But the harsher economic climate of the seventies has forced a change of mind, and in 1972 and 1973 — encouraged by the ILO report — the government took a series of measures which has brought Ceylonese consumers nearer to paying the prices goods were costing on world markets, and has simultaneously encouraged agricultural expansion.

Generally, a new spirit of realism is abroad. Mrs Bandaranike gave warning that 'we cannot continue merely to alleviate poverty without taking steps to attack its causes; we cannot concentrate on welfare measures while neglecting economic development.' And the new National Plan uttered some necessary truisms. It attacked 'an educational system which geared people to desk-type occupations and discouraged initiative and enterprise'. It added: 'The number of white-collar jobs which an economy can sustain depends on the growth of the productive sectors of the economy. It depends essentially, therefore, on the growth of agriculture, industry and fisheries.' Only common sense, perhaps, but courageous in the political circumstances. The government was uncomfortably aware that, at any probable rates of population increase between now and 2000, the population by then will have risen to between 20 and 27 million.

The situation is menacing, yet in some ways Sri Lanka's problems are the reverse side of her virtues. The political stability which has sustained democratic government when it has been collapsing in so many new nations has also produced a tendency to delay unpopular measures, such as the removal of the rice subsidy. The integrity of the civil service, compared with the widespread corruption elsewhere in the Third World, has been one of the reasons for the competitive nature of entry and the heavy emphasis on educational qualification: personal patronage must not be allowed to go too far.

Above all, as one local economist reminded me, the real

issue was whether his country could shorten the process of its development in a way which Western nations had never attempted. It had a per capita income of $160, he pointed out. When Britain had that size of income, its economy was growing at 1.5 per cent annually. Ceylon's was growing at 3.5 per cent, and indeed had had a growth rate of 4.5 per cent during the sixties, before the crisis engulfed her.

He also mentioned that Ceylon has a much more egalitarian distribution of wealth than most developing countries — in this respect, it follows the pattern of an industrial country; that its health and welfare services, as well as education, are well advanced; and that unemployment is partly caused by the raising of life expectancy during the past twenty years from forty-two to sixty-five. The death rate is now as low as that in the United States. Despite foreign exchange limitations, he added for good measure, 35,000 new jobs had been produced in a period of three years under a programme concentrating on activities requiring little capital.

The major effort, of course, is and must be in agriculture. One of the most encouraging days I spent in Ceylon was at a youth co-operative farming project on the road between Colombo and Kandy. The Nittambuwa Bandaranike Janawasa (people's residence) is part of an old coconut estate taken over under the land reform programme. Although the land formally belongs to the state, for practical purposes the twenty-nine young people there — mostly aged about twenty-four or twenty-five, though with some girls under twenty — operate it as a co-operative. At present they are paid a wage by the state corporation, but their profits go into a co-operative bank account. They use this to buy seeds, equipment and fertiliser, but they hope in a couple of years' time that there will be enough for a dividend to be declared.

Coconut production is said to be the lazy farmer's ideal. It is not quite true that you simply sit under the tree and wait for the nuts to fall on your head, but it is true that there is no crop which gives so many different products, ranging from liquor — the famous arrack, derived from the palm toddy — to a delicious salad vegetable found in the trunk. It is not, however, the most productive use of land, if you have plenty of labour available. So the young people have planted pineapples, bananas, passion fruit, coffee and soya beans. They also grow manioc, yams and sweet potatoes for their own use, and later they want to make treacle from the toddy extracted from the palms they have not felled. They would also like to keep livestock.

Most of these young people come from farming families, but their father's holding was not large enough to be split up further among his sons and daughters. So they live at home, in the three nearby villages, and travel each day to work. A few have married since the co-operative was formed, and in one or two cases the young couples are being given plots on the boundaries of the estate, where they can both establish their homes and act as watchmen on the farm at night.

Those I talked to seemed very happy with their new venture. One man of twenty said he had got as far as O-levels at school. If he had not joined the farm, he would have looked for a job in Colombo. But now he had concluded that he was as well off financially here, for fares, meals and city clothes would have increased the cost of working in Colombo, and he would also have had to face long daily journeys in each direction. Others who formerly worked in a metal factory and as a porter in a Colombo hospital also preferred farm life. But one youth who had had a job as a prisoner warder nearly lined up before he joined the co-operative, had eventually opted for the security of the government service. Tradition dies hard.

Agricultural experiments are going on all over Ceylon. Some young men have been given individual plots of a few acres, but climate and other factors have produced uneven results. Some earn as much as $1500, but one unfortunate in a dry area got only $120 in his first year. The government knows that it must do more about irrigation. A huge dam project will soon reverse the waters of part of Ceylon's largest river, the Mahaveli. This and other schemes will create nearly 200,000 acres of new farm land, and provide proper irrigation for another 200,000 acres that are already under cultivation.

Much of the new irrigated land will become paddy fields. From a point a few years ago when 70 per cent of the country's rice was imported, the government would like to be self-supporting well before the end of the decade. Rice output had already increased in the fifties and sixties; had it not, the foreign exchange crisis would have come earlier and would have been even more severe.

But sometimes the Ceylonese feel that they are swimming against a strong tide. One expert told me that the real agricultural revolution which is patently needed is only possible with more outside help than is forthcoming. About 20,000 young people have so far been settled on 46,000 acres of land. But it can cost up to 1500 dollars to settle one youth, particularly to give an educated boy the challenge of managing a real farm, which he can make self-supporting in two or three years. At present, such settlement schemes are only reaching a tiny sector of rural young people.

The government certainly appears convinced about the need for agricultural reform, even though it has found some of the ILO mission's proposals socially impossible. This applied particularly to redistribution of land among small-holders in order to create more economic units. What has proved even more difficult is the solution to the related problem of incomes and jobs. A revolution in the education system is now under way. In place of the educational steeplechase, consisting of a series of academic fences which eliminated most of the runners, school courses are being made much more vocational. There is a list of about eighty such courses, and the principal teacher chooses three or four suitable to the activities in his area – fishing in coastal areas, gemming in gem bearing districts, brick making, banana cultivation, and so on. The reformers feel that after years of educating children in the hope that they might achieve a place in Ceylon's élite, they are now really catering for the mass of children and preparing them for the kind of career they can actually hope to get.

But what is really needed to add a social and economic revolution to that in education is to transform the country's system of remuneration. The ILO mission wanted to freeze incomes in government employment, and in order to reduce its attractiveness to new entrants to pay them at much lower rates. But the powerful union for government clerical workers prevented that happening, and although real salaries for middle-grade government employees have been falling for some time, the revolution is having to be approached by a longer route.

The government is trying to raise farm incomes by banning the importation of some agricultural products which can be grown at home — chillies, onions, lentils and maize, for example. Faced by the sharp increases in sugar prices (which have helped other developing countries), Ceylon has slashed its sugar imports and thus encouraged the production of a local substitute, jaggery, which is based on the ubiquitous coconut palm.

Reformers hope that this 'change in the terms of trade between town and country' will convince young people before the end of this decade that they would be better off in agriculture. But it is admitted that at present there is still financial advantage for many boys who can force their way into the civil service. And old habits die hard: Only about a year ago, against the stream of educational and social thinking, someone introduced an O-level qualification for government drivers and watchmen. The hope must be that reform can be achieved before it is overtaken by some form of social explosion.

To reform itself, Ceylon will need more outside help than it is getting. One Colombo intellectual complained to me that while his country was adopting all the advice it was given that was at all practical — even to the extent of replacing its too lavish use of tractors by the more labour-intensive buffalo or ox cultivation — the real changes had to be made abroad. Above all, Ceylon must be allowed to process more of its own products, particularly tea, rubber and coconuts. And that brings us right back to the beginning: to the relationship between rich and poor countries, and to the international division of labour.

But Ceylon has still a lot more to do for itself. The country is immensely attractive. Its educated people argue endlessly about politics and ideas. I found myself one evening in the company of three brothers-in-law, who represented, conveniently, right, left and centre. As the arrack was served and the hot fish cakes and bananas were handed round by their wives, they argued the merits of the public service motive and the profit motive.

In a group of trade unionists, I heard a similar argument between those who want to attract foreign capital, and those — representing the Trotskyist union group which then supported the government — who argued that foreign capital could come for a specific purpose approved by Colombo but showed every sign of frightening it off by the most draconian plans for nationalisation of foreign estates.

Yet one is left wondering whether those solutions to Ceylon's problems which lie within the country are not simpler: in attitudes to work, in changing the reverence for desk jobs into admiration for those who produce on the land or in industry. A start might be made on the remarkable system of holidays, which is worrying the government. Because Sri Lanka is predominantly a Buddhist country, the Buddhist moon-day each month is a holiday. But so as not to discriminate, the festivals of the other religions are also free of toil: the Christian Easter and Christmas, Ramadan and the Prophet's birthday for the Moslems, and the various Hindu festivals. The colourful evening concerts around the lighted shrines to the Buddha, the ecumenical binges, with the arrack and other illicit forms of toddy, which mark the various New Years — all make it seem a pity that the government feels there is a case for fewer holidays. But when one adds the twenty-four days' annual leave and the twenty-one days' special holiday which the public service and much private employment offer, and throw in Saturdays and Sundays, one can see the government's point of view. Ceylon has some way to go to efficiency yet.

Perhaps it will not be as happy a place when attitudes have changed. I shall shed a tear myself when the educational system has changed so much that a rather tattered notice board will have to be removed from its corner on the Kandy-Colombo road, visible for a moment as my driver indulges in the national sport of passing buses on blind corners. 'Oxford College', it said. 'For your better scientific education.' It may be a pretentious way of describing an O-level crammer who can get you the necessary pass in maths at the third or fourth try. But it represents a strangely nostalgic society, reminiscent of a rather more gracious age. Foreign exchange difficulties and a genius for automobile engineering have combined to give the roads of Ceylon the appearance of England immediately after the war. British cars of that era are still running splendidly, and there are even a few Austin 7's from the thirties. Not the whole of the colonial heritage was bad, and there are many parts that independent Ceylon has improved upon. But there is a long way to go yet if all its people are to have a better life.

5 The Philippines:
a Crisis of Government

When President Ferdinand Marcos of the Philippines declared martial law in September 1972, observers felt that he had acted just in time to stop a deteriorating economic and social crisis exploding in violence.

'Marcos just succeeded in beating other revolutionaries to the draw,' said one young official in his administration, and since the political opinions he expressed were radical, I could not help wondering whether he might have been among the revolutionaries. His thesis was that Marcos himself, one of Manila's ubiquitous lawyers, with his origins on the fringes of the prosperous middle classes, has no real gut political position at all; he is neither on the right nor the left, but as a pragmatist he gained new insights into political and economic reality during his presidential years between 1965 and 1972. This was what made him act.

Someone with less need to be polite about the régime saw the situation in the context of democracy's growing difficulties in the Third World. The real issue, he argued, was whether the old politicians could adapt themselves and their policies quickly enough to avert an explosion of unpredictable dimensions which would sweep them all away. He confessed himself agnostic about the answer.

The Philippines story is of a country which could be prosperous but is fouled by corruption, socially divided by extreme and growing inequality and poverty, and with an economy which — for these reasons, among others — is rapidly running out of steam. Add a population explosion of Asiatic proportions, and it was obvious that something must be done. The Philippines government was another which elected to stimulate its internal debate on development by inviting an ILO employment mission. Its study and report, produced in 1974, fitted conveniently into a period when the Marcos administration was in the market for new ideas.

By the time the ILO mission, under Gustav Ranis of Yale University, arrived in 1973, it was estimated that more than a quarter of the labour force was either unemployed or underemployed. During the previous two decades, inequality had become worse. The share of income of the bottom 60 per cent of the population, the real rural poor, had actually declined from 32.8 per cent to 27.2 over the previous fifteen years.

This, in fact, was one of those societies where the dream of radicals in every age since Robin Hood — robbing the rich to feed the poor — was feasible. In all modern industrial countries, you could confiscate and redistribute the entire wealth of the rich without substantially improving the lot of the poor. But in the Philippines, you could double the incomes of the poorest one-fifth of families by reducing the incomes of the richest one-fifth by only 7 per cent. That is a measure of the degree of inequality in the Philippines.

Under the nation's system of democracy, no such radical distribution, nor even a more modest exercise, was likely to be considered. Both major parties, the Nationalists and the Liberals, represented vested interests, the big landowners and the industrialists. The congress, which they controlled, was a sink of corruption and patronage. Everyone in Manila now seems to have his story of wrongdoing under the old régime, and if even half of them are true a radical reform of the institutions had become inevitable.

The old politicians appear to have corrupted everything they touched. Elections at all levels were bought. The direct spending was considerable: someone estimated that it could cost as much as $140,000 to become even a councilman in Manila, so 'you had to be rich to buy people.' But public money was also used for patronage. One reason for cynicism about development programmes in many districts is that local politicians used to spend lavishly on ghost payrolls for supposed new public works schemes. Sometimes, particularly in the more remote islands, the community finished up with no road, or with one so carelessly constructed that it quickly collapsed, but with a large number of voters who felt a strong financial — and electoral — obligation to the incumbent politician.

Similar patronage existed in the central civil service. One senior official told me with delight how he had recently been able, apparently for the first time, to recruit men for an important new programme entirely on their merits. He had disregarded the names recommended by 'people with connec- tions'. If he had done that before martial law, he would have been dismissed himself. In the old days, to get an extra budget appropriation through Congress, you had to promise Congressmen to employ their protégés. He had once engaged a group of such people who had not bothered to turn up at the office except to collect their pay.

Even training schemes, desperately needed, were turned into useless election gimmicks: money was spent on courses like cosmetology and coiffure, which would win easy votes. As for land reform, it had first been launched in 1963, but nothing which would offend the big landowners in the Senate was done until after martial law was proclaimed. And the press? Why did it not reveal these scandals? Well, say the critics, not only were newspapers mostly owned by Establish- ment-minded people, but even individual journalists had silenced themselves by going on the payroll of important politicians, while still drawing a salary from their editors.

Corruption often took more violent forms. The Senate consisted almost entirely of lawyers. (Former American colonies, in this respect, tend to follow the United States.) But many of them were what American gangsters would call 'mouthpieces'. These men controlled private armies. They were euphemistically described as private security agencies, but I was told that they were 'sometimes better armed than the Army of the Republic'. Their 'soldiers' were employed to further the economic interests of those who paid their wages.

Often they acted as strike breakers, beating up pickets, driving away union organisers, and generally making life so impossible for the unions that one government official claimed that unions are better off now under the govern- ment's 'no strike' law: previously, because of prospective physical attacks, they had to find reasons for not calling a strike, while still maintaining the union's credibility.

Even if that sounds like a piece of special pleading for present government policies, the virulence of these private armies is not in doubt. I was told of union officials killed while trying to organise in a sugar plantation; of 200 strikers arrested during a textile dispute, after being manhandled by both the employers' 'goons' and the police; and of a newspaper strike in which drunken toughs were turned loose, armed with swords, on the pickets — later some pickets were arrested, and the strike subsequently collapsed.

In the fifties, the Philippines embarked on a growth path based almost entirely on protecting the country's small manufacturing sector from foreign competition. Only one in ten of the labour force worked in that sector, and the policy has been persisted in for so long partly because of the strength of the vested interests we have been discussing, partly because of the prevailing theory of development among newly independent countries in the fifties. This is now widely, though not universally, regarded as the wrong path. Industry was allowed to go for easy profits in the domestic market, aided by low interest rates, an over-valued currency and tax incentives. The money was drawn from a countryside blessed with good natural resources: exports include logs, sugar, copra, coconut, tobacco, pineapples and bananas.

The policy went well until about 1960, but then the cracks began to show. A swelling rural population found that there was no new land to be brought into cultivation. Even the Green Revolution helped the rich farmer more often than the smallholder, for the new strains of rice needed irrigation, and no one was providing irrigation for the small man. Rural incomes started to fall, and more and more people drifted off to Greater Manila, the honeypot where industrial jobs might be found — *might*. But because the domestic market was not expanding and because the industries had no incentive to compete in the more difficult international markets, they were no longer creating many new jobs. It was almost a classical case of what goes wrong when a government encourages capital-intensive industry in a labour-surplus society. Someone has estimated that it would take at least thirty years to cure the employment problem if the Philippines persisted in its old policy of concentrating on large-scale industry. Others say sixty years.

Why Marcos declared martial law is still disputed. Some say he simply wanted to perpetuate his own presidency. One cynical businessman, faced with the facts of corruption under the old régime, replied that present corruption in the army costs the country just as much but that it is not prudent to talk publicly about this.

Marcos certainly grasped that if he was to survive, the sluggish rural economy must be revived. The old politicians controlled most of the obstacles to this, and the President and the men around him knew that they must make a break with the Old Guard. One apologist claimed that the only freedom interfered with under martial law was the freedom of the powerful to exploit the masses. That is much too glib, but a more detached observer acknowledged that although the patronage system and the policies which flowed from it had not been destroyed overnight, there was an immense improvement.

The open opposition to Marcos now seems to be confined to the intelligentsia, who feel the loss of personal and political liberties most acutely. The oppression is not as severe as in many autocracies: for example, radical journalists are often invited to go abroad; elsewhere they would be imprisoned. But in the newspapers self-censorship seems to be widely practised, and the television companies appear particularly obseqious to what is called the First Family. Only in the Philippines, surely, would television miss showing a live world heavyweight boxing contest, which was taking place in a neighbouring capital, in order to record the arrival at Manila airport of the President's handsome, and highly political, wife.

The liberals have almost ceased to protest at martial law, because the mass of the people have voted overwhelmingly in referenda for its continuation. Law and order problems, which began with private armies, expanded into general thuggery. Not only were the city streets unsafe, but so were the villages. Rural support for Marcos is not simply on a law and order programme, however. Signs of development are at last appearing.

With the barriers of Congressional patronage removed, there have been more roads, irrigation, electrification, nutritional programmes and credit facilities in the past two years than in the previous ten or fifteen. The President, a shrewd politician, knows that safety lies in convincing the masses that he is moving things in their direction.

No one seems at all sure when, how, or even if the Philippines can work its way back to democracy. One visionary, who helped to form the abortive Nationalist Citizens' Party in the fifties to represent the have nots, believes that if free elections are restored in five or ten years' time, it will be possible to get political realignment. He is radical enough to think of a 'workers' and peasants' party' confronting the older groups.

His thesis is that the transfer of local decision taking from the old and corrupt barrios (councils) to the new barangays, which really represent the villages, has resulted in a dispersal of political and economic power from the few to the many, and that this cannot be reversed. He says the authorities are encouraging the formation of co-operatives, and that they are effectively strengthening the unions by urging them to unite. Don't worry about the suspension of the right to strike, he says. Once the unions are strong and united, no law will be able to withhold that right from them, for it is fundamental — the right to strike is asserted from below, not handed down by law from above. Meanwhile, as a fervent believer in trade unionism, he contents himself with the paternalism of state institutions to keep the workers happy.

Another less visionary observer put his faith also in the burgeoning strength of local institutions, though again in a somewhat paternalistic way. Local officials now have an efficiency audit, and are judged by their integrity and by what kind of development projects they are launching in their areas. Men who previously had an electoral incentive to lash out every last centavo on patronage employees are now holding back, and looking for activities which will really benefit their localities, and so impress the authorities in Manila.

Public health in the Philippines is improving. The infant mortality rate is low, tuberculosis is decreasing, and the population is growing at more than 3 per cent a year — an alarming rate. Add to this the fact that the land frontier has been reached — there is little more land which can easily and profitably be brought under cultivation — and you have the explanation of why people are drifting to the cities. There is no famine in the rural areas, but there is much malnutrition among children below school age.

There must be few Catholic countries in the world where family planning is so strongly advocated. One academic explained this by saying that many Catholics only go to church three times a year and are not very clear about the Pope's views on contraception. The Church nationally seems to be committed to the rhythm method — what one non-believer caustically called 'Vatican roulette' — but acknowledges other methods.

The family planning campaigners have tried hard. While I was in Manila, they had a campaign to place condoms in supermarkets, among the confectionery and chewing gum at the checkout points, so that they would attract the notice of shoppers. This ostentation offended a Catholic women's organisation, which threatened to boycott those super-markets taking part in the campaign. A moderate observer thought the family planners were pushing their luck a bit far: the condoms were less likely to reach married couples than to be bought by teenagers, attracted by the thought of free love but brought up in a society which had not prepared them for its pitfalls. When I left, the supermarkets were having second thoughts.

The Philippines may also be the only country in which the Department of Labour has introduced family planning into the labour law. Larger firms are required to provide advice and help for their employees. So far, birth control appears to be catching on quite well in large and small towns but to have been accepted less readily in rural areas.

With a population of 41 millions and a workforce of 14 millions, more than half of them engaged in agriculture, it is obviously important for the Philippines to be as nearly self-supporting in food as possible. There have been a number of false dawns as far as the staple food, rice, is concerned. One American expert said with admiration that this was the most sophisticated rice culture in Asia, apart from Japan and Taiwan. The Filipinos had taken to fertilisers just after the war, whereas in his previous posting, in Siera Leone, it was still difficult to get fertilisers accepted.

The Philippines also eagerly adopted the new varieties of rice produced during the Green Revolution of the mid-sixties. It helped, of course, that the International Rice Research Institute is at Los Banos, only an hour's drive from Manila and therefore conveniently placed for missionary work among the farmers of the 'rice basket', central Luzon. One sociologist was astonished at the eagerness of even the most remote farmers to get their hands on the new grains. In a village half a day's walk away from the nearest road, she found men asking for the latest variety, which had been specially bred to resist an insect, the brown hopper. Although the insect was not in their area, they were still determined to have whatever was latest!

In one season, 1969–70, the Philippines grew enough rice for its own use and even exported some, but swelling population and the limitations of the present irrigation systems overtook production again. Some experts say that with the spread of irrigation now taking place, allowing two crops a year instead of one, and given luck with the too frequent typhoons, the country could be self-sufficient in two or three years from now.

The government has put more resources into rice development than any other in Asia, for President Marcos is alert to the dangers of unrest if the rice supply is inadequate or too expensive; when there were elections, the price of rice was always a sensitive issue. Marcos has subsidised imported grain to hold the price down, and the farmers are also being subsidised through their fertilisers.

The ILO report advised the government to concentrate on irrigation and on introducing the high-yield varieties, rather than to rely on subsidy. Marcos accepted the advice, having already embarked on an ambitious irrigation programme, but when the petroleum price increase raised the cost of fertiliser, subsidies had to be continued to prevent a disastrous rise in the cost of living.

The ILO mission was aiming, through irrigation, at double

and treble cropping. The government enlisted the larger industrial firms in the operation by requiring major employers to provide some rice for their workers. Some companies have gone against expert advice and opened new farms in areas which are of marginal agricultural value, but others have given farmers valuable help with irrigation and enabled them to produce two crops in the year.

But when the ILO mission talked of rural development, it had more in mind than improving rice production, important as that is. The report sets out the vision like this:

> By 'balanced rural mobilisation' we mean the simultaneous growth of primary and secondary food production and of rural industry and services in a mutually reinforcing, self-feeding fashion. It is a mushrooming exchange of food grains, vegetables and poultry on the one side, and pumps, implements, shoes and shirts on the other, with the simultaneous generation of incomes and reciprocal markets.
>
> This mushrooming activity, with its generation of productive employment and output gains in a large number of small places, is not confined to an interchange of productivity between a town and its rural hinterland, but includes production and trading activities among the islands and between smaller towns and the intermediate level urban growth poles, as well as enhanced output-generating activity within a barrio itself . . . This vision of a dynamic and inter-acting rural economy is not just a romantic figment of the Mission's imagination. By international standards the Philippines stands well apart from the normal trend for a country of its size and income per head.

Both the government and others have seized on the idea of promoting rural industry with enthusiasm. The IRRI has shown how it can be done by offering its own designs for small agricultural machines free to local manufacturers. It has produced designs for tractors, threshers and tillers at as little as half the imported cost. Firms ranging in size between ten and 800 employees are using the designs, and are gradually driving out the more expensive imported equipment. Already they have won 70 per cent of the market for tillers from the Japanese, who previously supplied it.

The government is conducting feasibility studies into various low-capital industries, for example, the production of cheap rubber shoes and garments. There are also plans for more processing industries: it is hoped to sell more plywood and veneer furniture rather than exporting logs; and to turn coconuts into oil rather than allowing this to be done abroad. The construction of new feeder roads is also providing jobs, technical assistance teams are introducing new technologies to the countryside, and with the improvements in agriculture itself, the higher purchasing power of the rural areas should soon be a real strength to the Filipino economy.

But although the Filipinos are an enterprising people, the creation of rural industry is an uphill task, and it will take years to establish itself on any scale. One official told me sadly that of $70 million which the President had set aside for the purpose, only 10 per cent had been taken up.

This money was put at the disposal of rural and development banks throughout the country, and the President was considering whether loans could be made without collateral security. The Philippine's 500,000 Chinese compete with the banks as money lenders, but although they do not require much security, their interest rates are said to be exorbitant. (It is difficult for the stranger to know whether the stories told in Asia about the business activities of the overseas Chinese are truth or prejudice; they are talked about with the same venom as the Jews were in the Europe of Shylock.)

The government is also encouraging the creation of co-operatives, and is trying to persuade the trade unions to branch into commerce. It has had some success: unions are financing fish-canning, baking and meal projects.

All this represents a considerable revolution in Filipino thinking. Hitherto they have concentrated on cash crops, which had an assured market in the United States: as an American colony until the end of the Second World War, the Philippines had quotas for many commodities. That umbilical cord of assured trade is now being cut, and the Filipinos are having to think more about how to sell their sugar and other crops in the market places of the world. Mme Marcos has just secured entry to the Organisation of Sugar Exporters, and doubtless the dream of 'doing an OPEC' has entered several minds. The monopoly power of sugar is probably not strong enough for that, however.

The country also has to remember another piece of advice from the Ranis mission: don't concentrate so much on cash crops, mostly grown on plantations, just because the terms of trade happen to be temporarily favourable — as they were when the mission was in Manila — for in that way you risk throwing away the chance to develop the ingenuity of the majority of the rural population.

The part of the Ranis report which made the sparks fly, however, was that which affected the privileged groups in the Philippines, the owners of modern large-scale industries and the people who work in them. As ever, the tone of the international experts was kept comparatively bland, so perhaps for our purposes we may take instead a hostile summary of the report by the Philippines Chamber of Industries: '. . . industry has been made to appear as a spoiled brat, which took a larger portion of the pie during the import substitution heyday, and will have to be penalised, while agriculture and medium-scale industries take their turn.'

The mission certainly found that a quarter-century of protection had left their mark on attitudes among Filipino industrialists, causing them to look to the taxpayer, the consumer or the worker to subsidise the inefficiencies which inevitably creep in when an industry is protected too long from world competition. Put more positively, what Ranis was asking was that modern Filipino industry, instead of continuing to lean on agriculture for its capital, should turn outward and help to finance its own development by a major export drive.

It is important to understand that in suggesting a new growth path, the international economists were not simply peddling their own theories. Their view, that after twenty years of progress the Philippines' economy had reached a dead end, was shared by an influential group within the administration in Manila. This is confirmed by some sharp comments, after the report had been published, by Mr Blas

Ople, Secretary of Labour, who was President of the annual conference of the ILO in 1975.

He mentioned 'the paradox that, although the economy grew at a respectable 6 per cent over two decades, the poor became poorer, until growth must come to a halt because the people are too poor to support it'. This, of course, is the heart of the economic case for income distribution: that unless the ordinary people of a developing country grow more prosperous, there is a limit to the chances its economy has to grow. Not all the barriers are external.

Mr Ople deplored the fact that industries which were the major beneficiaries of import substitution, had

> refused to be weaned away from extremely paternalistic and over-protective policies; they came to enjoy and prefer an easy and comfortable life through public subsidies; they failed to exploit the opportunity to develop products that can compete in the international markets and thereby earn the means for their own further development and expansion; they remained, in effect, parasites upon the labour of sugar, coconut, hemp, and a few other cash crops turned out by the humble farmer and the migrant worker,

As an example of what went wrong, Mr Ople mentioned the garments industry. The Philippines has exported garments and embroideries since the 1920s, and some of the local products — shirts and blouses, for example — are very beautiful. But in the last decade South Korea has exported eight times as much, and Hong Kong twenty-two times. Ranis pointed out that the Philippines had two advantages: these two countries and Singapore, the exporting success stories of South-East Asia, were now short of labour; and the Philippines had greater entrepreneurial capacity than potential rivals like Indonesia, Malaysia and Thailand. He suggested that there should be a rapid expansion of exports in lines like garments, footwear, electronics, wood products (especially furniture), rope, metal products, knitted wear and toys. All these were labour-intensive. It was to help such industries to grow that he would like to see the peso remain undervalued.

The mission believed that Filipino industry could expand into world markets, that millions of people at present left outside the development process could be 'economically enfranchised'. It is estimated that four out of five people are not involved in any activity with real potential for growth. This is one of the roots of the Philippines' problem. If these people could be brought into development, living standards would rise, the growth rate could be raised to a steady 8 or 9 per cent by the end of the decade, and as income was better distributed the home market would gain in strength. Industrialists would still get profits — higher profits if all went well — but they would have to work harder for them.

Ranis and his colleagues knew that they were asking for sacrifices from industrialists and their workers, but they argued that if things remained as they were the system would eventually boomerang on the urban industrial class itself. Time was running out; the mission was offering a formula which would produce a better distribution of income, fuller employment, and higher growth rates.

Predictably, industry did not like the package, and it has been successful in persuading the government to change it beyond recognition. The mission wanted higher interest rates for industrial borrowers. In the course of a sustained debate, which was still going on when I was in the Philippines during the summer of 1975, the government watered down the interest rate proposals; although the rates have been allowed to rise a bit, they have not gone as high as Ranis proposed. Nothing much has been done about a proposal for a gradual reduction in tariff and other protection for industry, for reasons which will be explained in a moment. It was also proposed that tax incentives which favoured the use of scarce capital rather than of surplus labour should be reduced over a period of up to five years. What will happen to this proposal was still not clear. But it was clear that industry, for all the reverses it had suffered politically since martial law, was fighting a successful rearguard action.

Wages were also a problem for Marcos. In a guarded way, the mission had warned industrial workers that they would have to be patient until the labour surplus in the Philippines came to an end. Its principal remedy for social injustice, after all, was to ensure that more families earned a decent living by being brought fully into the labour market. That meant restraint by those already working.

So the report suggested that the government should subsidise rice and other essential foodstuffs if necessary, but avoid giving any automatic cost-of-living increase in the minimum and other wages, since these could produce Latin American levels of inflation. Some people in the Department of Labour in Manila always thought this an unrealistic proposal. The minimum wage had been fixed as long ago as 1970 at $1.33 a day.

In the event, it was not wages which fuelled the new spurt in prices. This, although not reaching Brazilian levels, was up to 34 per cent in 1974. Oil was the main culprit. The Philippines oil bill trebled in a single year, and the overall costs of imports, directly and indirectly affected by the oil crisis, doubled between 1973 and 1974. Marcos found it necessary to increase pay in the government service, and first to recommend and then to order private industry to do the same. But the wage increases have lagged far behind prices, and the Philippines, like many other countries, hopes to get its inflation back into single figures soon.

This was another example of how a sneeze in the international economy causes pneumonia in a Third World country. Yet another example was a recent fall in the world price of sugar, which caused a sharp cut in government spending programmes in the Philippines.

Indeed, the way in which the whole debate on a new path of development for the Philippines has been influenced by international factors is a fascinating study. Much of this book so far has been concerned with the internal policies of developing countries. This chapter has dealt with what the government, industry, agriculture, and labour within the Philippines might do to help itself. It is right to say that, even within the government in Manila, there are people who argue that the dispute which has engulfed the ILO mission's most controversial proposals is only about time-scale, that industry will accept the colder climate, provided it does not arrive with the speed of a Filipino hurricane.

I doubt the validity of this argument. What is certain is that some of those resisting the proposals for trade liberali-sation are doing so for reasons so fundamental to the international discussion of employment and development that it is worth setting them out at some length here, though they also form part of the final chapter. What follows is an account of the views of an economist who is associated with the business world in Manila. He is not philosophically opposed to the Ranis mission's ideas on the need for liberalisation of trade, but he is deeply sceptical about whether other countries will take much notice.

It's not an ideological confrontation. It's the developing countries against the industrial countries. They have the OECD and their various private discussion clubs. I simply don't believe we'll get free trade from the West. So we need protection to get our industries going.

I'm not saying that we should favour our own industry indefinitely. But remember that Japan, which is a near neighbour, is serving a domestic market of 110 millions. We have tyre companies here, and we grow our own rubber, and the Japanese don't, yet we can't compete against them without tariffs. We don't believe in making our country open to the world, and particularly to Japan.

It would be far better for us to build up our industrial potential together with Indonesia. Together, the two economies could be nearly self-contained. The way forward is for Asian countries to cooperate and complement each other's industries. If Indonesia provides us with 30 per cent of our oil, as is suggested, we'll give them fertiliser in return. That's the way it should work.

As for the industrial countries, we would like their technology and capital, but let them be invited to come here under conditions that we dictate. They must increase the local content of their companies, they must promote employment, and they must build up new industrial centres away from Greater Manila. This might not be attractive to Americans, but I think it would attract the Japanese. Supplies of raw materials are vital to Japan.

Please don't think from all this that I'm a diehard opponent of freer trade. I would lower tariffs case by case. But look, the Philippines is expected to reach a per capita income of about 600 dollars by the year 2,000. Now, it seems to me that 900 dollars might be a more probable estimate, but even so, remember that in the United States the figure is 5,000 dollars, and that in Spain, where they're still protectionist, the figure is about 2,000 dollars. Our present per capita income is only 270 dollars.

All this came from a man who was not a fool and had anything but a negative approach to his country's problems. He presented many coherent ideas for an alternative pattern of development to that proposed by the ILO Mission, ideas which diminished the role of government and enhanced that of private enterprise. For example, he wanted large national and international companies to be put under pressure by Marcos to spin off smaller enterprises. It was not easy to create small export industries, he said, for you needed a minimum of administrative mechanism. Rather than have scattered rural enterprises, you would be better to create eight or twelve large alternative industrial centres to Greater Manila, in order to get the benefits of the bunching effect.

'I'm against high taxation in order to finance new small and medium businesses,' he said.

It's unrealistic. The best talent in the Philippines is not in government, but in business. Competent men here get out of government and into business. We need fewer of our people going to the United States to pick up PhDs, and more of them going to pick up business ideas and technology, as the Japanese did after the war. We're still just a nation of traders, and we need to build up our industrial tradition.

As for income distribution, he acknowledged that much more needed to be done about that. Business would welcome more measures like the rice programme, which put an obligation on employers. More must be spent on housing, education and welfare services.

His general ideas, in other words, were nothing out of the ordinary; they may have been right or wrong, but they were argued in an intelligent and humane way. What was important, and I thought startling, was his assumption that nothing much in the outside world was going to alter, and that therefore the Philippines had better look after its own interests on that assumption. This was the *realpolitik* of the Third World. It is a view, of course, reflected among workers, industrialists and politicians in many Western countries also, and they will probably spend the remaining years of this decade 'looking after themselves' as well.

Ironically, it is the world inflation and recession, set off by the OPEC price increases, which is both the cause and the symptom of this mood. Countries which have been hurt — and everyone except the oil producers has been hurt — are turning in on themselves. Yet it was, originally, because the oil producers decided that only they themselves cared about their countries' future welfare, and therefore turned in on themselves, that the oil catastrophe engulfed the world. It reminds me, depressingly, of two political groups in my own country, Ireland. One, the Republicans, called themselves Sinn Fein, which is Irish for 'ourselves alone'. The other, the Ulster Unionists, have for long used the slogan 'what we have, we hold'. The determination of these two groups to look after themselves, to confront rather than to accept conciliation, has run through a century and more of Irish history like a malevolent thread, and the price for their intransigence is now being paid in blood and suffering. In blacker moments, while preparing to write this book, it has seemed to me that the West is saying: 'What we have, we hold.' And that the Third World is beginning to reply: 'ourselves alone'.

6 Agriculture: the First Step

If any dent is to be made in the world's poverty during the next quarter-century, it is in agriculture and the rural areas that the main changes must be made. The reasons are simple: that is where the vast majority of the poorest people live, probably as many as four-fifths of them; and that is where most of the extra food to feed the hungry must come from. Seen in retrospect, the concentration of most new countries since independence on their modern industry was an astonishing error in priorities. It was an attempt to move at one leap to the standards of living which the industrial countries had built up painfully over a couple of centuries. At best, it could only affect the living standards of a tiny fraction of their populations. But these people, of course, had most of the power and influence within the new societies. The silent majority of the rural areas were silent indeed.

The colonial powers bear some of the blame for the priorities chosen by the new régimes. Before independence, colonial administrators had also taken the greatest interest in industry and the large estates and plantations, for that was where European capital was invested. The peasants were left to their own devices, and they carried on their farming in the ways their peoples had used for many centuries.

To be fair, such neglect was not universal. I remember, on my first visit to Africa, meeting in Zambia a former British agricultural civil servant in the old Northern Rhodesian administration. He was by then managing a sugar plantation for a Zambian company, but before independence his job had been to encourage tribal groups to adopt farming methods which would preserve the soil from erosion. He was aggrieved that, since independence, the tribes had been allowed to drift back into their immemorial customs — to till the soil until it was exhausted, and then move on.

That was only one man's impression, but what does appear to be true, on a global scale, is that agricultural production in the developing countries is falling behind the increase in population. By the mid-seventies, food production per head was below the average level of the years between 1961 and 1965. While the rest of economy was growing, agriculture was falling back. During the summer of 1975, Henry Kissinger noted that the gap between the food that developing countries produced and what they need was already 25 million tons; that this would double or treble in ten years; and that unless we did something quickly, the world would face a series of increasingly unmanageable food crises over the next quarter-century.

Kissinger then announced United States support for a new agricultural development fund, which had been proposed by the oil states. He thought it needed $1,000 million a year. When one looks at the eating habits of the rich and the poor, and the effects these have on their health, both the vastness and the urgency of the problem cry out for drastic action. Barbara Ward and Rene Dubos in *Only One Earth*, the remarkable synthesis of the views of 152 international experts prepared for the Stockholm Environment Conference in 1972, said this:

> The bulk of the developing peoples with per capita incomes below 200 dollars were eating less than 2,000 calories a day, and the critical intake of protein was, on the average, not much above half that of the admittedly occasionally overstuffed inhabitants of the developed countries. These levels of consumption are simply insufficient for full health. The FAO has estimated that 300 million children in developing lands have 'grossly retarded physical growth'. Nor can we forget the retarding effect of protein deficiency on mental development.

That report contained a frightening account of how food production in the Third World was falling behind population growth, how families were having to exist on smaller and smaller patches of land, less able to leave it fallow, and so exposing it to exhaustion. There was limited scope for bringing new land into production: India, it was pointed out, was now cropping 402 million acres out of a potential 410 million. 'The only answer to this degree of pressure is a radical revolution in farming methods which, by increasing productivity, feeds the farmers, provides food for the workers moving to the cities, underpins industrial expansion, and helps to provide a lively internal market for manufactured goods.'

That was what ought to have been happening. And the reality? When the ILO reviewed the UN's Second Development Decade at the midway stage, in 1975, it found that in most Third World countries there had been no concerted attack on rural poverty and unemployment. Although it detected a break-down of the former reverence for the model of development represented by the industrial countries, the review saw no sign of an alternative strategy which would overcome 'the deeply entrenched structures of power and income inequality, which are inherently inimical to the pattern of development in which growth and equity become complementary'. And it added, with a touch of acerbity, 'Despite the avowals in plans and policy pronouncements, the directing centres remain more often than not essentially metropolitan and élitist in character.'

Not only for humanitarian and economic reasons, but for political ones also, this will have to change. Indeed, there are indications that a worldwide change in thinking is taking place, but many observers doubt whether it will happen quickly enough to prevent widespread alienation of peasants from their governments and, in some countries, even revolution.

The revolution in thought is slow. When former US Secretary of State Robert McNamara joined the World Bank as its President in 1968, the fashionable belief was still that what the Indians, the Kenyans, the Brazilians, and others needed was 'more horsepower at their elbows'. If they got that, they would raise their living standards by leaps and bounds. Those who did not see the immense possibilities of modern technology were reviled as Luddite. Agriculture didn't have much glamour; far better to help the poor to get into the towns and provide industrial jobs for them.

In retrospect, it was all so far from reality. In 1970 the industrial workforce of the Third World was only 13 per cent of the total workforce. The expansion of modern industry, even at the target growth rate of 8 per cent, could have little impact on employment during the seventies. Even by 1980, it was estimated, the countryside would still have to support 68 per cent of the population.

The UN's development strategy largely missed the point. Lip service was paid to the rural sector, but the planners drew most of their lessons from the obvious laboratory, the development of the advanced economies. They ignored the time-scale, the centuries in which the industrial countries got to their present position. Despite the new thinking, the UN was still advising developing countries to absorb an increasing proportion of their people in modern industries and services. That has to happen in time, of course; agriculture will employ fewer and industry more. But the UN, dominated by the understandable ambition of the Third World to get on terms with the developed nations as quickly as possible, was not honest enough about what was and was not practical.

Yet even within the UN system, there were strong contrary voices. A committee of experts, which met in Stockholm in 1969, entered a polite caveat about the usefulness of the conventional methods:

> The major problem of the Second Development Decade is likely to be unemployment and underemployment which, if not forcefully attacked, could easily reach half the labour force of developing countries by the end of the decade. Employment is the foundation on which all other objectives of development rest. Moreover, given the limits to capital accumulation and the nature of present day technology, there is little hope of 'structural change' in developing countries as a group, in the sense of a rising share of the labour force fully employed in the industrial sector. Nor is there hope that the absolute numbers employed in agriculture will fall.

So that was the crisis: if present policies were persisted in, half the people in the Third World might be unemployed or underemployed by 1980. We would not be progressing in our attack on poverty, but sliding back. Slowly the penny began to drop: there had to be a sharp change in direction. The new thinking began to appear in the ILO, whose country employment missions concentrated more on the problem of getting rural people into more productive work; in the Food and Agriculture Organisation, which became increasingly preoccupied with the sheer size of the world population we were going to have to feed; and in the World Bank, where McNamara and his officials began to see the urgency of a change.

One of the decisive influences on the new thinking was McNamara's own travels through about seventy-five of the developing countries. Because the World Bank dispenses money, either on 'hard' or 'soft' terms — and now through a third, intermediate 'window' also — its officials are not content to visit capital cities, but like to take a close look at what is going on in the places where its projects actually are.

One official summed up the impression they got in the famous words of Abraham Lincoln: 'God must have loved the poor, he made so many of them.' If there was to be anything which could be dignified by the word 'development' in the Third World, it must mean helping the poor to be more productive, and therefore able to support themselves. The poor lived for the most part in the countryside and worked in subsistence agriculture.

The Bank's lending programme was transformed. The emphasis now was on the elimination of mass poverty through agriculture. Most money was directed at those in the bottom 40 per cent of the population. There was a determined shift away from capital-intensive projects, which would help a small number of people, and towards projects benefiting many small farmers and others living in the country. By using quite small amounts of money in labour-intensive projects, the Bank was able to help, directly or indirectly, many more of the poorest. The money mostly went to fertilisers and the simplest of machinery and equipment.

The ILO, acutely aware of the social side of development, realised that time was short. Nothing was moving fast enough. The report for the World Employment Conference in 1976 drove home its belief that the changes needed were radical, even revolutionary, and that they would probably be obnoxious to the power élites in some developing countries. The best way to reduce poverty within the next twenty-five years, it was argued, was through a radical redistribution of both assets and income; it was the only way to get self-sustaining growth which really affected the whole population. That meant major changes in land ownership and tenure. But in many parts of Africa, unequal access to water, credit, markets and other services was often as great a handicap to the poor as their lack of land.

Even in some densely populated Asian countries, credit and water were almost as important as land reform. But in much of Latin America, a redistribution of land was the inescapable first step. Indeed, a study commissioned by the World Bank and the Institute of Development Studies at Sussex University concluded that in Latin America a redistributive land reform could go a long way towards a solution of rural poverty within a relatively short period. Many Latin American countries, unlike most of those in Asia and Africa, were colonised by metropolitan powers which were feudal rather than capitalist. As a result, they are still handicapped in their rural areas by a feudal structure. The differences between some modern *latifundia* and the slave plantations in the United States before Emancipation is not great.

But reform in Latin America is more a political than an economic problem. That applies to other areas also, though everywhere the circumstances are subtly different. In many African countries, for example, what is needed is for more of their educated men, economists and agricultural experts, to go and live in rural areas and help to make small farming more efficient by their advice and leadership. One project in the Nigerian countryside employed experts from three different international organisations for two years, but found it hard to get the limited number of qualified Nigerians to live in the backward areas, where there were no schools for their children.

For the educated African, the call of the cities is strong, for he suspects — and at present he is right — that promotion lies there. Perhaps only salaries which differentiate in favour of the rural areas, or even mandatory service there, will solve the problem.

Throughout the Third World, this reluctance of educated men, the natural leaders, to work away from the cities is an obstacle to rural development. One Asian, working for an international organisation, was more blunt than any European would have dared to be:

> In many Asian countries, they have sophisticated machinery of national planning. They have produced good plans, and yet quinquennium after quinquennium the results are not there. In India, corruption is only part of the story. The problem seems so vast that they have not come to grips with it. So many people are profit-oriented that social considerations are very secondary. They will bribe officials and so on. We need fewer planners, and more practically trained men prepared to work in the countryside. Many of the planners are working on false statistics, because when urban-educated people are asked to do rural work, finding out what's happening in rice production or family planning, they simply make the answers up. So you don't need to take much notice of those fancy computer results; they have no relation to reality.

Another man, a European, put more of the blame on the international organisations. He said there were too few middle-level managers and local leaders for rural development, and too little international effort to produce them. He believed the planners who made the frameworks in the Third World were efficient, but that the middle link was missing — the technicians, overseers for road gangs, and so on. Until they existed, rural development would not work. Governments must be prepared to commit funds to their rural districts.

Some observers, taking up the point that the problem is more political than economic, argue that Third World governments will only get the necessary support to override the strong vested interests of the rich if they mobilise the rural poor in associations or unions to fight for a better share of national resources. Mr Raj Krishna, in his presidential address to the Indian Society of Agricultural Economics a few years ago, put the case for militancy strongly. He attacked the inefficiency and corruption which had attended many Indian reform schemes, and gave warning that the government could pour money into the countryside without increasing productive capacity or transferring income significantly. He said:

> Instead of reducing the poverty and idleness of the poorest, it may further enrich the rural oligarchy and bureaucracy, and increase inequity and tension in the countryside . . . The unemployed, the landless, the crop-sharers and the insecure tenants must be organised into militant unions to demand that project funds and benefits really reach the poorest, and are not swallowed up by contractors, rich farmers and petty bureaucrats . . . Without militant rural unionism, laws and policies have not benefited and will not benefit the mass of the rural proletariat.

Mr Krishna believes that governments only respond to people who put pressure on them. The tragedy of the rural poor of the world is that, whether their countries are colonies or independent, they have had little political influence. Yet with populations growing, and the conventional development policies manifestly failing to keep pace, events may give them a terrible new power — that of sheer desperation. It is hard to avoid the conclusion that, in country after country of the Third World, those in control are — or at least ought to be — racing against a time-bomb of revolution.

This is not to imply that the solutions are easy, even if the will existed. In Asia, for example, there is a scarcity of land relative to population. It has been estimated that in India, even the transfer of 43 million acres from the largest landowners would only reduce the proportion of country people below the poverty line from two-fifths to one-third. The absolute figure of people who would be helped is large, of course — between 20 and 25 millions — but the reform would still leave between 80 and 100 million Indians landless. Faced with a problem of this scale, it is scarcely surprising that land reform in India has been much talked about but not often acted upon.

Yet reform there must be. In what direction? The international agencies take some care not to be politically identified with any one system, for their constituency is divided by ideology. But the examples of Tanzania and China keep coming into the conversation when agriculture is under discussion. There are flattering references to the Ujamaa programme and to the Chinese communes. Other countries — Kenya and Bangladesh, for example — have made interesting, but limited, experiments in dealing with rural poverty, underemployment and stagnation. But there is a strong feeling in the West that the rich and powerful groups in such countries are not likely to reduce their own wealth to help the poor. Looking at the Chinese Communist performance, some staunch parliamentary democrats fear that the choice presented to millions of the poor in many countries will appear to be 'bread or liberty'; and that if it is presented in that form, they will inevitably choose bread.

The disastrous harvests of 1972 drew fresh attention to the world grain problem. In 1974, when Robert McNamara discussed the subject in a speech, there was a reasonable long-run balance of supply and demand in the world as a whole, but this was only because of high productivity in the great grain growing areas, notably the United States and Canada. Grain yields in the Third World were only 40 per cent of those in developed countries.

If things went on as they were, the poor countries would be trying to import 70 or 80 million tons of grain by 1985, and that would cost them $20,000 million in foreign exchange. There was only one answer: they must be helped to produce more grain for themselves. McNamara urged developing countries to use irrigation to expand their cultivated areas, to increase their use of fertilisers, and to maintain a price structure which would give local farmers an incentive to produce for domestic markets. He acknowledged that money for expansion would have to come from the rich nations. The extra plants for producing the amount of fertiliser needed by 1980 would alone cost between $6,000 million and $10,000 million. And while the Third World was using all its available money for investment in agriculture, the West and others would have to subsidise its higher import costs of petroleum, food grains, fertilisers and manufactured goods.

Ordinary citizens in the West, even those with kind hearts, are often so numbed by the scale of world poverty that they close their minds to it. If you are worried about how to find £30 in London, or $65 in New York, to pay your gas bill, it is difficult to focus on McNamara's demands for $10,000 million. Yet in agriculture, in particular, a little money goes a long way. Oxfam, the British-based voluntary aid organisation, sent £900 in 1966 to a co-operative in a Mamfe village in the Cameroons. In the first two years, this money was used to buy tools — saws, axes, machettes and spades — as well as fertiliser and sprays. Thirty-five acres of dense rain forest and scrub were cleared and planted with 300 palm oil trees. A year later 5000 germinated seeds were in the ground.

The idea of co-operative effort and the new agricultural methods quickly caught on. Two more villages joined the scheme, resources and equipment were pooled, houses and wells built, and new forest areas were turned into plantations. Three years after the co-operative started, Oxfam sent it another £3500 for new tools, seeds, sprays and fertilisers. For these two tiny sums of money, the people of these three villages now have work throughout the year. They are building up a new life for themselves, and migration to the towns has stopped.

Ten years ago, the accepted wisdom was that Third World farmers should be helped to adopt the mechanised methods of the West. There was some grassroots resistance to this, along original Luddite lines, by people who believed their jobs were being put at risk: in the Argentine, an Australian harvester was blown up, for example. It is now widely agreed that to use expensive tractors in places where the shortage is not of labour, but of capital, is a foolish waste of resources. It makes even less sense to spray crops from a helicopter or light aircraft when there are many idle people looking for work.

The way in which premature mechanisation has driven unnecessarily large numbers of peasants into the cities, most of them to exist in squalor and poverty, is another of the tragedies of mistaken development policies. Development experts now mostly accept that agricultural improvements must fit in with existing social and economic structures. Even mainly subsistence farmers may sell some of their produce, but the small amount of money they earn is needed for absolute essentials — salt and sugar, clothing, and a little oil for lighting. They simply do not have cash for expensive equipment. One of the most fascinating aspects of new development policies is the search for the most suitable technology for primitive farmers.

In a recent experiment in Tanzania, an ILO expert, George Macpherson, and a Cambridge economist, Dudley Jackson, found natural resistance to expensive change: 'Everything you tell us to do costs more; how do we know we will get it back?' It was, as they acknowledged, a sound piece of scepticism. Tanzania's income per head in 1971 was $92, one of the lowest in Africa, and putting it among the world's twenty-five poorest nations. About 94 per cent of the people live outside the towns.

To suggest to people existing in such grinding poverty that they should use mechanised methods, which would cost eighteen times as much as their traditional oxen, would be madness. But there were simpler methods by which the burden of life could be eased. President Julius Nyerere said recently, 'Our women still carry the crops to market on their heads; ox carts or donkey carts are still so rare as to attract attention, despite the large number of these animals which are eating our fodder. This situation must be changed . . . The Ministry must act rapidly to make improved tools available, and the farmers must press forward and use the new methods.'

The village technology experiment aimed to do just that. Macpherson and Jackson were determined to build on the skills which existed. Previous attempts to introduce mechanisation had required the constant attendance of government employees, such as agricultural engineers. When they went away, the machinery tended to fall into disuse because it was not properly maintained.

'To avoid such failures', Macpherson and Jackson wrote,

innovation should start at the current level of technical competence of the village people. In most villages there are men skilled in the use of the axe, the adze, the panga and the hoe. In many villages there are carpenters who make chairs, tables, beds, doors and houses, using these implements, while in some there are smiths who forge adzes, hoes, knives and other small tools. This provides a reservoir of basic (mostly woodworking) skills, which could usefully be tapped by the project.

They grasped the essential point, that they must substitute wood for metal wherever possible. They must use materials that the villagers themselves were accustomed to — tree trunks, bush poles, planks, nails, bolts and nuts, corrugated iron, scrap iron from old vehicles, discarded rubber tyres and tubes, leather and rope. This was the basis of the village technology they created, a determined effort to avoid the processes which could only be carried out with outside help. The wheel, that historic symbol of man's progress, is as good an example to take as any:

> It is not necessary to construct an iron-spoked, iron-rimmed wheel, because adequate wheels can be made by cutting two layers of planks, laid at right angles to each other, into a flat circular disc, fitting the disc into an old rubber tyre, and then nailing the planks to each other and the tyre to the planks. A wooden axle can then be made and fixed rigidly to the wheel. Inserted into wooden bearings containing plenty of grease, with reasonable maintenance and the periodic application of more grease, such a wheel and axle function efficiently. In the case of a breakdown, the repairs can be done on the spot by the villagers, unlike a metal wheel, which may require welding.

To some Third World politicians — in my view, the less far-sighted — such descriptions of how their people are being asked to accept what they regard as second-best technology are still offensive. They crave the shining machines of the West. As we have observed before, psychology, as well as economics or politics, comes into this argument at every point. The economics of appropriate technology, particularly in agriculture, are right. But how do you deal with the psychology? Does it help to say that every agricultural people has traced the same steps?

While I was writing this chapter, I described to my wife the Tanzanian experiment, and particularly the wooden wheels. In childhood, she had spent much more time in the Northern Irish countryside than I had, for her grandparents lived there. She gently deflated my wonder at the Tanzanian production of a wooden wheel, by recalling that many of the farm carts she knew in Ireland thirty-five years ago had wooden wheels also, though of a somewhat more elaborate construction. They could be repaired by the local carpenter. It will be a tragedy if a misplaced political dignity in any way obstructs the first steps in agricultural progress which the new ideas can promote. The north of Ireland has many tractors now; its agriculture was mechanised somewhat more rapidly than England's, in the end. But the wooden wheels served their purpose well at a time when money for repairs was scarce.

No one is suggesting that Third World agriculture should have a dogmatic commitment to simple methods. Even among the extreme poverty of their Tanzanian village, Macphereson and Jackson advised the villagers that they would be wise to buy the simple iron ploughs which are on sale in Tanzania, rather than make do with a less satisfactory wooden one which could be made more cheaply in the village. One advantage of village technology is that it can save the peasant's money to buy those implements which have a real advantage.

But the lesson which the authors drew from their experiment is one for politicians as much as for development experts:

> The pressing need in the Third World today is to expand agricultural production, especially food production, and such expansion must take place on a broad front, involving all farmers, especially the peasant or subsistence farmer. Unfortunately, to many people development still means projects planned on a large scale, but with benefits confined to relatively few. It is therefore encouraging to discern a steadily growing interest in projects of smaller scale but with more extensive coverage, and it is not

accidental that this concern is accompanied by a growing awareness of the need for greater equality in the distribution of the fruits of economic development. One might coin the motto 'small is egalitarian'.

Rural development, like farming itself, is a matter of infinite patience. An OECD expert has estimated that it will be between ten and twenty years before we see the full fruits of the changes now beginning to take place. Robert McNamara has acknowledged our ignorance about the practicalities of bringing improved technology to hundreds of millions of small farmers, and about the costs.

'But we do understand enough to get started,' he says. 'Admittedly, we will have to take some risks. We will have to improvise and to experiment. And if some of the experiments fail, we will have to learn from them and start anew.'

One of the countries from which much is to be learned is China. One does not need to be an admirer of Maoist ideology to think so. Unfortunately, the Chinese still let visitors see only what they wish to show. There can be no question of the rest of us learning from their mistakes, for every effort will be made to keep them from us. China remains, despite recent relaxation, the most effectively closed society in the world. Her reluctance to give information about grain harvests and prospects, as the world's planners worry about whether this planet can produce enough grain to feed its starving people, is a disgrace. What about the Russians, the Chinese might reply, pointing to the Soviet buyers slipping through the back door of the Chicago grain exchange. You-tooism cannot excuse the refusal of both countries to co-operate, except on their own terms. It makes a mocking hypocrisy of their grandiloquent professions of international brotherhood.

But the world cannot afford to be proud about learning from the remarkable Chinese rural experiments. Nowhere is this more true than in public works. One of the inefficiencies of subsistence farming is that between harvests the peasant often does not have enough work. In Kenya, as we saw in an earlier chapter, the building of feeder roads has both improved the rural infrastructure and provided cash incomes for country people with time on their hands. In the Tanzanian experiment described above, farmers who mastered the skills of making farm implements have gone on to improve their homes by making more furniture for them.

What the Chinese have shown is that rural public works can be organised on an enormous scale, and by labour-intensive methods. The size of their population and the almost military discipline of the Maoist system may mean that their methods are only conceivable in a large, totalitarian society. But what has aroused the interest of research workers in the ILO's World Employment Programme is the way in which China has adopted the principle that available rural labour time is a precious asset which can be used to raise productivity and make more goods and services available. Adapting the principle to the non-Maoist world, the ILO would like not only to improve rural amenities, but to provide the landless labourers of poorer developing countries with the only cash income many of them are ever likely to have.

The other great break-through in rural development is double-cropping. The new hybrid strains of grain are, for all the disappointments which have surrounded the Green Revolution, a bright gleam of hope for hundreds of millions of people. Agricultural research is a vital part of any plan to feed the world's poor adequately. One of the useful outcomes of the World Employment Conference may be the creation of a network of regional, national and international research units for appropriate technology. This would not be confined to agriculture, of course, but there is little doubt that its most important impact would be in the countryside.

The ILO staff is suggesting a small international unit, with only twenty or thirty professional staff, so that most of the work can be done through national or regional institutes, thus keeping it close to the realities of the Third World. One suggestion is that governments could tax multinational companies to pay for such fundamental research. Six broad areas of inquiry have been suggested: manufacturing and processing activities related to food; solar power and other small-scale sources of power; the design of simple farm implements; the development of equipment for lifting and moving water, especially pumps; brickmaking technology; and the use of traditional materials in building houses, village schools, etc.

Already there are nine or ten specialist institutes, operating under the wing of the World Bank. They cover such research fields as semi-arid crops, potatoes, wheat and maize, livestock, root crops, vegetables, and — perhaps the most famous — rice. Because such work is so fundamental to our hopes of feeding the poor of the world, the next chapter will be devoted to the Green Revolution, and in particular to the attempt to make the rice eating countries of the world able to feed their swelling populations.

An overwhelming proportion of research and development still occurs in rich countries, because that is where the highest profits are to be made. One expert suggested to me that it might be as high as 98 per cent. Why, he asked, instead of catering for the vast markets of the developed world, could some research effort not be devoted to providing cheap refrigerators, which would lighten the lives of peasants in the steaming heat of their tropical poverty?

Again, one comes across the obscenity of the choices. How do you justify employing scarce scientific manpower in the West to discover how to put stripes into toothpaste, when in the Third World it could be engaged on the most fundamental advances like, for example, the Biogas development in India, which has produced both fertiliser and energy from animal and human waste?

7 The Green Revolution

Rice is the staple food of the poor of the world. Not all of them depend upon it, of course, but it represents more than half the food of one-third of mankind, 1300 million people; another 400 million have it as an important part of their diets. And the people who depend primarily on rice enjoy an average annual income of only $80.

It was because of these startling figures that the Green Revolution, the scientific break-through of the mid-sixties, which produced higher-yielding grains, sent a shiver of excitement round the world. Were we about to get the chance to cure the hunger which afflicted or threatened hundreds of millions of human beings? Just as the frightening tide of population increase was threatening to engulf man, had he been saved by a miracle?

If you use the word 'miracle' at Los Banos, in the Philippines, the home of the International Rice Research Institute, it brings a frown to the face of the scientists. 'Miracle rice' was a too glib journalistic description of IR8, the first successful new strain of rice which the institute revealed to the world in 1966. The scientists there feel that the phrase has rebounded on them, that they were credited with having solved all the problems of mankind, when all they had done was to take a significant step forward.

IR8 may not have been a technical miracle, for its limitations became apparent as it was tried in different countries; it did not suit farmers who had no reliable supply of irrigation water, nor those who could not afford larger quantities of fertiliser; and it did not suit the palates of many Asian rice eaters. Yet in a political sense, it was 'miracle rice', because the way in which its fame went round the world

convinced farmers, scientists and politicians that rice production could be transformed. Since then, there has not been so
much difficulty in persuading governments and international
bodies to provide funds for agricultural research.

When the Ford and Rockefeller foundations decided in the
late fifties to launch the IRRI, average rice yields were about
1.5 metric tons per hectare, which was what they had been
for centuries. Yet in some temperate countries, like Japan,
farmers were getting two, three or four times more than that.
One of the reasons was that peasants in the tropics did not
have the option, like the Japanese, of using large quantities of
fertiliser, for this caused the already tall rice to grow even
higher, and since much of it became ready for harvesting at a
time when typhoons are prevalent, the risks of finishing up
with a flattened paddy field were too great.

What was needed was a short rice with a strong stem,
which would not fall over when a lot of nitrogen was applied.
If the plant could be made to stand up, it would use the
nitrogen to produce more and plumper grains. In trying to
produce such a rice, the Los Banos scientists made thirty-
eight crosses. The successful one involved a tropical semi-
dwarf variety from Taiwan and a traditional Indonesian rice
which resisted insects and disease well. This eventually
produced a yield of 6.6 metric tons per hectare. The Green
Revolution had begun.

What made this development particularly exciting was the
ever-growing need for more rice. So fast are populations in
the rice eating countries increasing that demand is expected
to be one-third greater within the next ten years. The balance
between supply and demand is always precarious. Bad
weather in 1972 doubled prices generally, and trebled those
in some countries. As usual, the poorest were hardest hit: in
the Philippines, for example, the worst off, who were already
spending 37 per cent of their pitiful incomes on rice, found
that they would have to spend 74 per cent if they ate the
same amount. For hundreds of millions of rice farmers,
engaged in subsistence agriculture on a few acres, the yield is
vital. But it is equally important to landless labourers and to
low-income workers in villages, towns and cities.

IR8 was only the beginning of the Green Revolution in

rice. It was followed in 1967 by IR5, which was more suitable for drought conditions. But pests and disease were also problems, and among the new strains which appeared in the next few years was IR20, which could produce higher yields with less insecticide and in poorer soil than other varieties. One of the criticisms of the Green Revolution was that it benefited most those farmers who could afford large quantities of fertiliser and insecticide. Indeed, some people have at times seemed to regard it almost as a counter-revolution, because it favoured the rich against the poor, and encouraged a large landowner to take in more land, mechanise, and drive more small men off their land. As we have noticed before in this book, matters rarely work out exactly as planned. One critique of the effects of the Green Revolution suggests that the new rice was used in only a little over one-tenth of the rice growing land of the world, and that as output increased, labour was widely displaced as more capital-intensive technology was introduced.

It would be foolish to blame such retrogressive steps on the men who found the new rice, which is undoubtedly a blessing to mankind. The scientists at IRRI are aware of the social consequences of their discoveries, and they keep trying to find new strains of rice which will suit all possible circumstances. Eight in every ten hectares of the world's rice are grown without irrigation. Both upland rice and rainfed paddy have exceptionally low yields, whereas in irrigated fields, where the soil can be kept under water, there is less trouble with weeds and soil disorders. Research into these matters could be of immense benefit to the peasant farmer, who usually has to wait for his government to provide him with irrigation. IRRI, knowing the tardiness of many governments, is looking for quicker ways to help him control disease and insects, get reasonable yields despite drought or flood, and grow rice on poor soils.

The institute has a vast programme of research, involving tens of thousands of different strains of rice from all parts of the world. It is now seeking not a single 'miracle rice', but a variety of types which will give high protein levels, tolerate drought, toxic soils, deep water and cold, and resist diseases and insects. This huge germ plasm bank forms the basis for the Institute's genetic evaluation and utilisation programme.

The piece of research at Los Banos which I found most intriguing was the attempt to create a variety of rice which can give high yields in areas where floods during the monsoon season would ruin the semi-dwarf varieties. Perhaps as much as half of the world's rice is grown in such conditions. They cover the great river valleys of Asia — the Ganges, the Brahmaputra, the Godavari, the Irrawaddy, the Chao Phraya and the Mekong. Men have lived in these valleys for thousands of years, because their soils are fertile and because there is always enough water to grow rice.

But floating rice is the only food crop that will thrive in these valleys and deltas. The water often reaches a depth of between 1 and 6 metres, and over the centuries the floating rices have developed genetic mechanisms which enable them to grow normally even when the water is deep, because they elongate their stems as the water rises, allowing their leaves to float on the surface. Sometimes the harvesting is actually done from boats.

But the yields from floating rice are only as good as those from lowland varieties of the era before the Green Revolution. If something could only be done to improve those yields, some of the poorest people in the world would be helped to grow enough for their families to survive the famines which have been the scourge of such areas.

What gave the impetus to the present programme of research on rice suited to flood conditions was an accidental happening in August 1974. The first international seminar on deep water rice was to be held in Bangladesh — at Joydepur, 35 kilometres north of Dacca — towards the end of August. But in the weeks preceding it, flood waters covered two-thirds of Bangladesh, destroying much of the rice and affecting about 30 million extremely poor people.

Most delegates expected that the Bangladesh Rice Research Institute would cancel the seminar, because of the appalling difficulties of organising it under such circumstances. But a wise decision was made to go ahead, and as a result, the visiting scientists had a chance to see, from boats, from the air, and on foot, the devastation, crop destruction and human suffering that flooding can cause in the low-lying areas of Bangladesh, as in other Asian countries. (Burma was suffering severe flooding that year also.) The visitors were shocked by what they saw, and quickly recommended that there should be an international task force to stimulate research into the problem. It arouses the imagination when you have seen rice growing to a height of 5 metres in flood water.

Rice crops in such low-lying areas are often submerged for up to a month. What the scientists are attempting to do is to incorporate genes from the floating rices into the semi-dwarf and intermediate varieties, with the intention of making them both flood-survivors and high-yielding. The experiments continue. Rices from Sri Lanka, which have adapted themselves over many centuries to survive periods under water, are among those being used.

Only one-fifth of the rice lands of the world, where water depth is between 5 and 50 centimetres, are suitable for the high-yield varieties so far discovered. Simultaneously, the fight against cold is going on in another part of the institute. And the fight against cost. Because of the high and increasing price of insecticides, fungicides, herbicides and fertilisers, the research staff at Los Banos are trying to find ways of doing the same jobs with nature's aid. Local rices which already grow in adverse conditions are being studied, and the scientists will try to use their relevant genes in place of expensive man-made substitutes.

The latest experiments when I was in the Philippines were with early-maturing rice varieties, which were high-yielding and resisted the major insects and diseases. They grew in as little as 105 days, compared with 160 days for traditional varieties. Such speed of growth will allow small farmers to grow either several crops of rice or to have other cash crops as well.

In the tropics, the growing season lasts throughout the year, if the farmer is organised to exploit it. One of the tragedies of Third World development at present is that the fertility which nature gives in soil and climate is often squandered. In the very poorest countries, it is worst. In Los Banos they hope that many more families in Asia and Africa will soon be supplementing their diets and perhaps their incomes with such crops as sweet potatoes, soybeans and vegetables — provided they can get a really suitable variety of rice.

No less than one-third of the world's rice is produced in China. Again, the extraordinary isolation of the largest nation is part of our story. When the Director of IRRI, Dr Nyle C. Brady, went to China in 1974 with a group of American plant scientists, he reported that the Chinese claimed to have released a locally developed semi-dwarf variety of rice in 1960, from a genetic cross made in 1956. The Chinese were also quick to test the IRRI varieties. They tried IR8 only a year after its release, and Dr Brady saw fields of his latest variety at that time, IR26, growing near Nanking; it had been sent to the Chinese the previous year by President Marcos.

As détente proceeds, the world may hope to get fuller benefit of the remarkable Chinese agricultural experience. Dr Brady brought back with him forty Chinese rice varieties and outstanding experimental lines. They are being included in the IRRI breeding and testing programmes, and there will be strong pressure from the outside world for China to co-operate with IRRI's research.

It is not known for certainty whether rice originated in China or India. Men definitely cultivated rice in China at least 6000 years ago, and the country is now the world's second largest exporter, behind the United States. As with other crops, the most diverse selection of rice varieties is likely to occur near the region where it originated. This is one of the reasons why rice scientists, now that the Bamboo Curtain has been lifted, are anxious to use China's great wealth of rice germ plasm.

They are also impressed with Chinese farming methods. Through changes in these methods, the Chinese now grow two crops instead of one, often another food crop. Even in the famous communes, they are moving to small-scale mechanisation to relieve production bottlenecks. Their two-wheel hand tractors, which are like the IRRI tiller, are being manufactured and used on some communes. But like the rest of the world, China is short of fertiliser, and even though compost, made of rice straw and animal and human wastes, is applied, some rice fields have nutrient deficiencies.

But if the Chinese have their problems, it would be wrong

to suggest that the Green Revolution has solved, or even is in sight of solving, the problems of other rice growing countries. Ward and Dubos, looking at the subject from the standpoint of their concern with ecology, are clearly worried about the side-effects of the Green Revolution. Because improved seed, fertilisers, and water supplies require higher investment of capital, they fear that only the big farmers will benefit.

The fifty-acre man in Asia, the 10,000-acre man in Latin America can hope for a larger return on his investment if he consolidates holdings, terminates tenancies, heavily mechanises his operations, and turns loose the subsistence farmers or sharecroppers who scraped a living from his land before fertilisers, new seeds and insecticides gave him both the chance of higher returns and the need to secure them in order to cover capital costs.

If the authors of *Only One Earth* are apparently pessimistic, it is because they see the Green Revolution going wrong, not technically, but socially or politically: men being cleared off their land in India and Pakistan to make way for the tractors, the ecologically sound agriculture of the small man being challenged. The real issue is whether the new farming methods which the Green Revolution has given us can be combined with sane land reform and co-operative investment policies to produce a countryside which will both feed and employ its people more adequately. The Green Revolution is not so much a victory of Man over Nature as a challenge to Man's good sense.

8 In the City Slums

The informal urban sector: it is one of those examples of economist's jargon which brings a grey glaze across the eyes of the layman. Yet this is one of the most colourful, exciting, bizarre, sometimes squalid, but often amusing aspects of Third World development. It is the bustees of Calcutta, with ten-storey blocks of flats squashed into the gardens of older houses; the favellas of Rio, tumbling down the city's many hills, under the shadow of the vast statue of Christ, yet an affront to the millionaires and bathing beauties of Copacabana and Ipinema; the slums of Nairobi, living permanently under threat of death by bulldozer; the incredibly crowded back streets of Hongkong.

This is the story of people who have left the countryside, usually driven out by poverty, the population explosion and the land famine. They have arrived *in* the city, but are not yet *of* the city, for it has offered them no job. So, singly or in families, they set out to make what kind of living they can. They are hard to define, and no one can ever be quite sure when a man is informally urban — or urbanely informal, perhaps? — and when he has crossed over into 'that undiscover'd country from whose bourn no traveller returns' — no, not in this case the Hereafter, just the modern economy.

However, acknowledging the difficulties, economists have made a stagger at defining the characteristics of the informal urban sector: ease of entry; reliance on indigenous resources; family ownership; small scale of operation, with no more than ten or fifteen workers; technology which is labour-intensive; skills that are acquired outside the schools; and unregulated and competitive markets. Add two negative qualifications — that governments offer it few favours, by way of import licences, equipment subsidies, credit, or low interest rates; and that they often harass it legally — and you have a fair idea of the informal urban sector.

The international planners have now set out to convince the authorities in Third World countries that this sector has great potential for growth, and that it has a much better chance of providing jobs for the ever-growing populations of the metropolises of Asia, Africa and Latin America than has modern manufacturing industry. The scale of the problems certainly demands some radical change in direction, for if urban poverty continues to grow at the rate of the past quarter-century, there is serious danger of violence and civil upheaval. The poor in the cities are more combustible material for revolution than are those in the countryside.

It is estimated that about 200 million poor people live in Third World cities. The number is growing all the time. In 1950 there were only sixteen cities in the developing world with populations above 1 million. Now there are over sixty, and by the end of the century the number will probably have risen above 200. Half of the urban growth is due to population increase and the other half to migration from the countryside.

In the past generation, there has been a move into the cities of the developing world on a scale the world has never witnessed before. The towns and cities of the rich world grew at a much more leisurely pace, and they were able to absorb their new citizens with greater ease. Probably 400 million people in this generation have moved into cities, and it has been estimated that by the end of the century three out of four people in Latin America will live urban lives. The growth of Rio and San Paulo appears unstoppable. One out of three Asians and Africans will also be in cities by the year 2000. The frightening fact is that the great conurbations of the Third World may have to absorb another 1000 million people. Yet already half the people in the cities of India are undernourished, and a quarter of the child deaths in the African cities are from malnutrition.

Already the modern sector of the Third World cities can only provide jobs for about two out of five of the people who live in them. The wage earners in formal manufacturing industry are in the top half of the population. Any visitor from an advanced country must quickly begin to turn his definitions on their heads. For example, the 'self-employed' label in Europe often conjures up visions of some privilege — a professional man, perhaps, with more chance of extra earnings (and of tax avoidance) than the salary earner. In Africa, the self-employed person is likely to be somewhat lower on the social scale than a street sweeper.

For self-employment can take many forms. Those who have defined the informal sector are sensitive about emphasis on the occupations which may unjustly reduce its economic significance in the eyes of outsiders. Yet Harold Lubell, who has done the principal ILO research into that most remarkable of cities, Calcutta, is catholic in his definition. He includes not only the long-established and astonishing small engineering workshops of Calcutta and Howrah, but also the one-third of the population who carry out 'all those low productivity tasks that keep the city moving, eating, and as clean as it ever is — cooks, domestic servants, watchmen, peons, bearers, sweepers and scavengers, rickshaw pullers, porters, washermen, gardeners, waste paper collectors, etc'.

And with a nice touch of scholarly detachment, he adds a question of national accounting theory: whether incomes earned in begging, prostitution and theft represent productive income 'or merely income transfers'. It is a problem which has not been satisfactorily tackled by accountants in the developed world either.

People working in this sector of the economy sometimes have low productivity, they may be described as underemployed, and they are often looked down upon by their own governments. But it should not be thought that they are idle or work short hours. There are men in India prepared to stand at a roadside for sixteen hours a day with a bicycle pump, in the hope of earning enough to eat by pumping up other people's tyres. There are scribes at Indian post offices, sometimes equipped with typewriters nowadays, instead of pens, ready to write letters home for those migrants who are illiterate. There are men selling single cigarettes to passing motorists, hanging around for many hours on street corners,

and still offering a light to their customers as an extra piece
of service and inducement to buy. There are traders willing to
stand on the streets of Nairobi from dawn till well after dusk
for the barest livelihood.

These Samuel Smiles principles of self-help, however, do
not impress many legislators and officials of the Third World.
Governments often regard the sector as backward, inefficient
and a painful reminder of a less sophisticated past. This is
incredibly short-sighted. Even on the most hopeful estimates
of growth in world trade and in the manufacturing
industries of the Third World, there is no prospect that
development and poverty problems will be solved in that
way. All over the developing countries, the informal sector is
providing large numbers of the newly urbanised with what
livelihood they can scrape for themselves: nearly half the
population of Lima, more than half that in Bombay and
Jakarta, and over two-thirds of the people in Belo Horizonte.

The informal sector also enshrines much of a developing
country's real hope of growth. Japan, for example, is a story
of the successful exploitation of this sector. The Japanese,
when they were building themselves up from defeat after the
war, were prepared to develop the most complex system of
sub-contracting — just as had been done in Calcutta a
generation and more before, and in England and America
several generations before that again. So far, many of the
developing countries have not seen this opportunity.

It is true, of course, that there are industrial areas where
the informal sector cannot compete with heavy capital
investment. But small family firms can often compete in such
areas as food, clothing, furniture, packaging, repairing and
servicing. The small man, with his motorised rickshaw or his
gaily painted Filipino Jeepney — the most bizarre development of war surplus stock, surely, that has ever been seen —
can often beat a transport combine for price and convenience
to the passenger.

As for housing, the ILO reported recently that a Tanzanian
informal construction group, working by labour-intensive
methods, could produce a six-roomed house for $700,
whereas much smaller houses built by the housing corporation would cost more than twice as much.

It is difficult to analyse fairly the Third World antagonism to developing the informal urban sector. Partly, of course, it is the tendency, which has been noted earlier, to ape the developed economies. Yet industry and commerce in Europe and North America progressed along similar routes. In the Industrial Revolution of the nineteenth century in England, 'putting out' of work, particularly in textiles and clothing, to people who worked in their own homes was an essential part in the growth of industry.

One international expert argued to me that while the Japanese economy had been a caricature of the Western model, its meteoric success could be fully explained by its ability to use the small men, creating what economists call linkages with the tiny sub-contracting firms who made a living on the fringes of urban society. He further argued that Hong Kong, Singapore, Korea and others were successfully following the same path. Why couldn't other developing countries see that this was the surest way to get their exports off the ground? They had a price advantage in textiles, shoes, clothing, some parts of electronics, and in other goods where the labour content was high. Of course, he conceded that tariffs and other forms of protection were a problem, but those were matters which could be argued about if they first set out to encourage and build up such industries. At worst, they could produce cheaper and better goods for their home markets.

What is being missed by the neglect of these small manufacturing concerns is the opportunity to nurture in-genuity and enterprise. These are qualities which must be encouraged if formal industry and commerce are to grow, rather than rest on such laurels as they have. The examples of ingenuity and enterprise are many. The ILO first dramatised the concept of the informal urban traders in its Kenya report, though their existence long pre-dated that report. Kenya already had people making cheap shoes out of old tyres. In Pakistan there was a man who employed a dozen or so people to make implements. He financed himself in the early stages by getting his customers to pay for their goods when they were ordered, and he made a handsome profit which allowed him to reinvest heavily and grow rapidly. In Abidjan, in

Nigeria, families with sewing machines were holding their own against factories in the ready-made clothing trade. In Ceylon, a bewildering variety of artefacts were reaching the export markets — wicker baskets, black elephants, even a million walking sticks to meet an order from Germany.

Such manufacture may sound trivial to the Western businessman, as it does to many politicians and officials in the capitals of developing countries. Both the multinational companies and the people who welcome them to the Third World sometimes barely seem to acknowledge the existence of small firms which can make a serious contribution to national development. They are important for capital accumulation, their overheads are low, and they offer a personal incentive to build up a business.

Yet it is the large enterprises that are given advantages through exchange rates which encourage capital imports, special tax exemptions, under-priced public utilities, and subsidised interest rates. Sometimes this is a matter of corruption. Many multinationals, perhaps through necessity, have been willing to give backhanders to politicians or officials. But often it is a myopia which extends to all the activities of the poor.

For despite the socialist rhetoric which appears almost obligatory in large areas of the Third World, we here encounter again the obscenity of internal inequality. It is an inequality in absolute wealth and in opportunity which would be quite unthinkable in the industrialised world. It is an inequality and a willingness to do nothing about it which leaves hundreds of millions of the world's poorest people with neither the hope nor the opportunity to rise above the most abject levels of existence.

You encounter it in ways which are significant both for people's personal living standards and for the long-term economic development of their countries. For example, public services. Many of the people who live in slum areas of the great cities in the developing countries have no access to public water or sewerage. They may pay a street vendor of water twenty times the amount that much better off families pay for a water supply which is piped into their homes. Yet the authorities would probably tell you that they have 'a minimum standard water supply of 200 litres per person each day'. So they provide that for the more affluent sections of the city, and leave huge areas without any water or sewerage facilities at all.

Not only is this a cause of personal discomfort. Many slum areas are riven by cholera and other diseases because of inadequacies in water and sewerage. Yet the health services are often geared also to the richer groups in the community — elaborate modern hospitals, instead of the small local clinics which could deal with elementary health precautions concerning hygiene and diet. Similarly, in education, the schools reach only the better off families, when what would benefit the most children is the provision of small, cheap schools which would teach basic literacy and arithmetic and give vocational guidance that had some relation to the real employment possibilities of the children.

The ILO's preference for a basic needs philosophy is applicable to the urban slums. Its experts are suggesting that governments should concentrate on housing, water supplies and sanitation. Instead of plumbing the individual homes of the well off, why not put communal water taps at quarter kilometre intervals, and in some cases provide neighbourhood washing and toilet facilities? The ILO also sees the need for studies of systems of sewerage that would be cheaper than water-borne methods, and might also produce waste in a form which could be used to supplement chemical fertilisers.

To talk like this, of course, is to run against the stream of modern technology that many Third World governments delight in. Often, under the influence of their own economists and of multinational companies, they import a complete package of technology from advanced economies. It will take a lot to persuade them to begin the kind of experiments in appropriate technology which, it is generally agreed, are more likely to help their poorest people.

But nowhere is the attitude of authority to the poor shown more clearly than in the field of housing. People have come to the cities in the hope of finding work. They therefore want to live close enough to places of employment to take a job. Yet about 70 per cent of them cannot afford the cheapest public housing. The result is that they build their own crude shelters — from packing cases, cardboard, corrugated iron, old advertisement hoardings, anything which comes to hand. Again, the ingenuity is astonishing.

Some of these homes are hovels. It must be admitted that many are health hazards (though principally because of the lack of water, sewerage, and rubbish disposal facilities). Some are even more dramatically dangerous: in Rio, the favellas are erected on such perilously steep slopes that in rainy weather they sometimes slide down, and people have been killed and injured. But it is no solution for the city authorities to clear away these eyesores and force their inhabitants to live an hour or more's bus journey away from downtown Rio, where they might hope to get a job.

As I write, the most appalling piece of inhuman bumbledom is reported from Dacca. In January 1975, Sheikh Mujib's government apparently decided that it must clear out the bustee squatters who were crowding into the business centre, almost to the doorstep of the Inter-Continental Hotel. So they transported 100,000 people to three camps ten to fifteen miles away from the city, presumably so that there would be less temptation for them to come back. One of the sites was below flood level. None had anything but the most primitive sanitation.

Oxfam, the aid agency, described conditions in the camps as some of the worst they had seen anywhere in the world over three decades. More than half the children under five were suffering from severe malnutrition, and about thirty a week were dying of starvation. Oxfam, helped by the British government, was rushing out sixteen simple sanitation plants 'to get the excreta off the ground'. The fatal illnesses of the children — apart from simple hunger — were mostly water-borne, diarrhoea and worms, which were going almost directly into the local water supply.

How does a government get itself in such a position? The almost incredible poverty of the whole of Bangladesh is part of the answer. Doubtless corruption is another part. But the underlying reason is that many Third World countries are still run entirely by and for the middle and upper-income groups. There is a disdain, or rather almost an oblivion, which enshrouds the plight of the poorest people. For all the limitation of social attitudes in the advanced world, such callousness would now be impossible: people cannot be treated quite so badly by the most thoughtless governments, if only to avoid serious civil disorder.

Because of the immensity of the problem, it is understandable that some governments have either averted their gazes, or adopted solutions which would be more appropriate in Birmingham, Sydney or Chicago. Send the bulldozers in. Clear the slums. Maintain health and planning standards. This is splendid, provided you are in a position to provide alternative accommodation at a cost the displaced people can afford. But there is no question of this. Too often, the government has nothing to offer. The poor are simply left to start again, on some barren site, far from jobs, and with the few pitiful facilities they had created for themselves destroyed.

There are several other methods of dealing with such slums. One would be to upgrade them. It is argued that if governments would only give tenants security by promising not to sweep away their shanty homes, private initiative would make most of the improvements needed. One estimate is that 80 per cent of city people could improve their shelter without public subsidy if standard regulations were lowered. It might be better still to provide sites with basic amenities, and leave the slum-dwellers to build for themselves.

What is needed, in housing as in general attitudes to the urban poor, is a complete change in direction. The better off – workers in commerce and industry, the middle classes, the rich – have nearly all the political clout in developing countries. Can governments muster the courage to tell them that they will have to pay more for their water, sanitation, electricity, roads and other public services in order to create parallel services for the slum dwellers? In the long run – when the poor have bus services which prevent their having to spend up to two hours walking to work, when their education and health and housing are sufficient to support a decent standard of living – the whole country will benefit. Productivity will rise, and everyone's living standards will rise with it. But in the short term, what is needed is a drastic redistribution of income and wealth in favour of the poor.

All the money that can be raised in taxation, from trade and in aid must be devoted to improving the services to the poor. They need help to get small enterprises going in the slums. They need industrial sites, buildings, access to credit, an end to bureaucratic obstruction and delay, an end to licensing rackets, to unnecessary regulations, help in creating marketing co-operatives — in fact, a general feeling that the government is on their side.

That is the doctrine that the ILO, the World Bank and other international agencies are now preaching to the Third World. They have come to the conclusion that many governments have biased their policies against the poor, whether inadvertently or not. The way to put this right is now understood. It ought to be acted upon, and though lending agencies like the World Bank can do much, the enthusiastic support of Third World governments will also be necessary.

Some people think the best pressure point would be on the multinational companies. The reasoning goes like this: it is not as easy to create an export industry from small beginnings as the idealists think. You need the marketing and managerial expertise of big organisations. So don't start from scratch. Force the multinationals — by regulations, incentive payments, or fiscal penalties — to be less capital-intensive, to sub-contract more to the small men, to provide them with training and technology, sell off second-hand machines cheaply, let a man work in the factory for a time and then establish his own small business.

Perhaps the multinationals can be persuaded to be the driving force in the search for an appropriate technology for the Third World. Already Phillips has a pilot plant at Utrecht which plans its move into a developing country with more care than many multinationals have shown in the past. Too many multinationals just move in, take advantage of tariff protection and cheap labour, and ship out as much of the profits as possible. That is no way to benefit the receiving country. The multinationals are susceptible to much sterner bargaining.

The Philippines has had some success in this direction in its handling of the car makers. Five foreign companies have accepted terms that require them to build up local industries which provide components. But government regulations aside, some of the more far-sighted international businessmen see other reasons for welcoming a move in this direction. First, several surveys have suggested that the smaller businesses are often more efficient. But second, if markets in the Third World are ever to become attractive outlets for multinational companies, they need the massive build-up of their small enterprises which will create better living standards. Even long-term self-interest ought to encourage the richer countries to help.

9 The International Dimension

We have been preoccupied in much of the earlier part of this book with what I have called the first obscenity — gross inequality of wealth and income *within* the developing countries. So far most of the discussion has been about policies which individual governments in the Third World could adopt to improve the lives of their poorest people. It is now time to turn our attention to the second obscenity — gross inequality *between* the rich and poor countries. Most of the international conferences concentrate on this second subject, and the Seventh Special Session of the United Nations General Assembly in September 1975 was felt to have made a break-through on the New International Economic Order, which the developing nations had been demanding for several years.

Just because there is this concentration on the international dimension, it seemed important in this book to emphasise that the national and international remedies for world poverty are complementary, not alternatives. Neither will work without the other. It would be possible, for example, to achieve a New Order internationally and yet to leave many millions of people little better off, if the international changes are not accompanied by national policies of redistribution and equity. The risk is that richer nations may make this fact an excuse for doing nothing. But the most enlightened policies by national governments in the developing countries will not work unless the developed nations display realistic generosity. What is needed is a massive trade-off, informed by a mixture of decency and self-interest, which will produce new policies both nationally and internationally.

What needs to be done internationally often appears immensely complicated. After a time, the layman feels like closing down the shutters of his mind as the suggestions and demands proliferate: for commodity agreements (but single or comprehensive?), for buffer stocks (but how financed?), for indexation of import and export prices, and so on. It becomes simpler if we start from the objective, which is to alleviate poverty and to bridge the immense gaps between the advanced and developing nations in the remaining years of this century. The most hopeful way of doing this appears to be by seeking a new and more rational division of labour in the world, and that can best be achieved by removing national obstacles to the working of fundamental economic laws.

Let us admit at once that this is not the best moment in all history to tell Western industrialists and trade unionists that the world will be a finer place if they allow goods to be produced where costs are lowest. It is easy, after all, to change the direction of a car when it is moving, but hard to turn the steering wheel when you are standing still. The industrial world is now in the depths of the worst recession since the 1930s. The Keynesian verities are under assault, and there is no alternative economic consensus. It is not surprising that attitudes are conservative rather than dynamic.

As I write, a newspaper cutting lies on my desk. A little of it is worth quoting:

> Textile workers' leaders [at the British Trades Union Congress] angrily demanded government action to help the hard-pressed textile and footwear industries... The Congress carried a resolution regretting that the Government had rejected a broadly based appeal from the textile industry to control the imports of foreign manufactured textiles at a rate of 20 per cent lower than those imported in 1974. The Government should seek to control imports of textiles, clothing, knitwear, and leather goods from low-cost countries, and also apply quota restraints against areas of unfair competition.

Fresh from the appalling statistics of Third World poverty,

it is tempting to sneer at such language. But to do so risks failure to understand the complexity of the issue. For example, one of the speakers at the TUC challenged the British government's warning that import controls would bring retaliation, by pointing out that Britain had a trade deficit of many millions of pounds with countries such as Hong Kong, Taiwan and South Korea (which are among the better off in the Third World). No one mentioned the ethnically sensitive but economically significant fact that many of the workers whose jobs in British textiles the unions were seeking to protect were born in India, Pakistan and Bangladesh, which are much poorer.

Migration of workers is, indeed, one of the more bizarre workings of the international economy since the Second World War. It is a measure of our failure to achieve a rational economic system, and it may be a symptom of a deeper human mood of conservatism, which will be worsened by the recession. Yet what the world economy appears to need is radical structural change. This is only likely to come about when developed societies have confidence in themselves, and that confidence is sadly lacking at present in many Western countries. If one were asked to name the least well understood piece of damage done by the oil crisis, this loss of confidence would be it.

Mood is important. When workers have personal experience of changing jobs in mid-career and moving up the skill and earnings ladder, or when they have seen their friends successfully doing so, no great problems arise about adjusting to the decline of older industries which cannot face the competition from low-cost countries. But when the mood is defensive, trade unions instinctively resist change, because they know that other jobs will not be available. This produces a vicious circle, for as structural change occurs too late, too slowly, and on too small a scale, unemployment does indeed rise and living standards fall. It is a kind of self-fulfilling prophesy, and the mood of failure and of defensiveness is reinforced.

Structural change will only come about when working people in the West, and the unions who represent them, are convinced that 'upward mobility' is a real possibility and not just an economist's abstraction. It will come when they firmly expect an increase in world trade, with the extra purchasing power generated in the Third World by the transfer of resources and jobs also creating new and better paid jobs in industrialised countries.

What cannot be doubted is the illogicality of how the system works at present. Developed countries erect barriers of protection around industries in which their capital is often inefficiently tied up. This prevents developing countries supplying them with the same goods more cheaply, but it does not prevent the influx of workers from poor countries to provide the labour of which the same industries may be short. The remittances these migrants send home have been described bitterly as 'crumbs from the rich man's table', yet in economic terms they are significant. In the early seventies, the remittances from Europe alone amounted to more than all the aid of the World Bank. Small wonder that a note of despair crept into the tone of one ILO expert, W.R. Böhning, as he contemplated this Mad Hatter's scene:

> It cannot be the purpose of a rational international division of labour to import raw materials, workers, and to some extent capital for labour-intensive production lines in industrialised countries, when this very process retards trade-determined structural change, jacks up the price of consumer goods, impedes employment creation in developing countries, and puts the burden of the process largely on the shoulder of the migrating workers.

How much of the burden of our illogical world is being carried by migrants and the families many of them leave behind? In a way, they *are* the new international division of labour at present. Take North-Western Europe, the outstanding example of large-scale migration in the post-war world. There has been a steady influx of people in that period from the Mediterranean littoral — Spain, Portugal, Italy, Greece, Yugoslavia, Turkey, Morocco, Tunisia and Algeria. France and Germany, with their booming industries and labour shortages, have been the principal targets, but all the countries of this prosperous corner of the developed world have received their share. In Switzerland's case, it is much more than her share: one worker in every four in Switzerland is an immigrant.

It is impossible to be precise about numbers. There were probably about 6.2 million immigrant workers in continental North-West Europe at the height of the boom in the early seventies. With families added, this made more than 11 million immigrants. Commonwealth immigration to Britain is in a somewhat different category, but if you add the British workers and families of overseas origin, the grand total for the Common Market and adjoining countries may be as high as 13 or 14 million.

Look at this, in the first place, from the viewpoint of the immigrants. Economically, they have gained, and that was why they came. Most have attained standards of living beyond their dreams in their own countries. But as they and, more particularly, their children settle in, they begin to realise that they are still at the back of a queue, this time the queue for the better jobs, promotion, status and educational opportunity in their new country. Frequently they are fobbed off with work that the natives do not want — heavy, dirty, dangerous, unpleasant or monotonous. It is also usually the less well paid work.

On top of all that, they may well have to cope with an uncongenial climate, ethnic and racial prejudice in personal, social and work relationships, and legal restrictions in such matters as work permits, which will effectively restrict their freedom of choice, put them at a disadvantage in the labour market, and may even thwart attempts to reunite a family they had hoped they were leaving behind only temporarily. It is not surprising that, as one Asian put it to me, most immigrants hope eventually to lay down their bones in their homeland, even if few of them actually contrive to do so.

What the recession of 1975–6 has begun to show is the essentially exploitative nature of the relationship between the host countries and immigrants. An ILO document says the immigrants are treated as 'a reserve supply of labour'. It points out that in time of recession, the migrants tend to lose their jobs first and are often sent home, thus 'providing an anti-cyclical cushion against unemployment for national workers'. It has been estimated, for example, that in West Germany during the 1966–7 recession, about 30 per cent of the migrant workers left the country, not always voluntarily;

and that in the present, and much deeper, recession, the figure is already 20 per cent and rising. In one twelve-month period spanning 1973 and 1974, Germany exported unemployment of about 300,000 jobs.

Migration has long been an emotional subject. In Britain, for example, the argument has broadly been between those of liberal pretentions, who believe that this ought to be a multiracial society, welcoming people of different national and ethnic origins, and that opposition is largely a matter of colour prejudice; and those who argue that immigrants would be better off in their own countries, and that — more particularly — British jobs and social conditions would be safer if they had never come. A catch-phrase — 'they've come here to take our jobs and women' — has been created to caricature the most illiberal minds.

It is a shock to discover that the repatriation argument, usually the preserve of racial bigots, can also be derived from the demand for a new international division of labour. It runs something like this: Is it not ludicrous that textile factories in the parts of the north of England should be so largely manned by Indian or Pakistani immigrants, when they could more happily do the same work in their home countries, if only international trade was free? And can one justify bringing Turkish or Yugoslav workers to German factories (in many of which they form a third or even a half of the production-line labour force) when if only the world could organise itself to take the work to the workers, they and their own countries would be more prosperous and more content.

The influx of migrants has effects for workers in industrial countries. It may help them to escape some of the less pleasant jobs, but often it depresses wage levels. Perhaps the outstanding example of this is in the United States, where the arrival of illegal immigrants from Mexico has kept wages for Mexican-American farm labourers at deplorable levels.

In industrialised areas also, the low wages acceptable to immigrants have had their effects. Again, a depression of the general wage level, at least in the lower reaches of the labour market, is one result. Another is to save, at least for another few years, labour intensive manufacturing industries which the law of comparative advantage might otherwise have transferred to a developing country. Industries like textiles, shoes, electronic assembly and food processing are the most notorious examples.

So ought all good liberal minded people to change step and declare themselves against migration? It is not as simple as that. This is another case — there are so many in discussing Third World development — where the best is the enemy of the good. Ideally, of course, industries would move to whichever country best suited them: where wage rates would enable them to produce as efficiently and cheaply as possible. In doing so, they would save millions of people from the hardship and heartbreak of economically enforced exile. Theoretically, too, such a move should lead to cheaper prices for consumers, although competition is not always so perfect as the economists suggest and the effects of lower production costs often disappear into the pockets either of manufacturers, middlemen or retailers.

But, looking at it again from the standpoint of a possible migrant, the most cogent argument against waiting patiently to be rescued at home by a more perfect international division of labour is that it probably will not happen. We are back to the argument used by the business economist in the Philippines: in a world of total free trade and rational decisions on all sides, of course, the sensible way to behave is this and this. But in the imperfect world in which we actually live, you must do the best you can for yourself.

That is what the immigrants are doing. In the Maghreb countries, for example, the per capita income in 1971 was only one-tenth that in France. The temptation for an ambitious, or desperate, man to migrate was great. The same relative advantage applied to Turkish workers contemplating a move to Germany. Even a dirty, boring job, which no one in the European country wants, may be preferable to the best job open to them in their own country.

So the well intentioned, if bewildered, liberal must still be against closing borders to migrants (though that is what is happening more and more in Europe, as the recession deepens). For closed borders without a radical international redistribution of industry just mean that developing countries have to support more of their people, without the benefit of the remittances that migrants send home to their relatives. When one realises that in even a comparatively prosperous country like Yugoslavia, remittances accounted for more than 10 per cent of total personal spending in 1971, the severity of such a blow can be guessed at.

Yet the distorting effect of migration cannot be ignored. It appears in many strange forms. For example, Western Europe actually increased its exports of textiles, clothing, footwear, and electrical equipment during the sixties, while the migrants, who could as easily have worked at making such goods in their home countries, poured in. And the migrants were self-selecting, with all the harmful effects that can have on a developing country. Often it is not the unemployed who decide to seek a better life in Europe, but those trained men who are already in jobs, and have enough self-confidence to risk leaving their own country. But their departure reduces its efficiency, and it may well make an employer who has trained them more reluctant in future to rely on labour which may leave. Thus the pressure for labour saving techniques gets another turn of the screw.

This skill drain has been almost as damaging as the more notorious brain drain. If only underemployed agricultural workers had left, the economies of the Third World countries concerned would have benefited, especially as the remittances flowed in. But a survey of Turkey, to take one example, shows that the country's huge agricultural sector has supplied few of the migrants, while construction, shipbuilding, coal-mining, and textile firms saw their labour forces depleted by the exodus. Even in the migration from Fiji to New Zealand, it was foremen, mechanics, electricians and building workers who left, while farm labourers mostly stayed at home.

There is understandable reluctance in the Third World to take draconian measures to control emigration. How can you tell some of your citizens that you're ending their opportunity to earn a better living abroad, without first being sure that you will one day be able to offer them something as good at home? There can be no such certainty, for there are at least two dangers. One is that, if migrant labour was all miraculously withdrawn tomorrow, the industrialised countries might simply raise their tariff barriers higher to offset the higher wages they would have to pay to native workers. There might be little or no relocation of industry. The other risk is that, even if a new international division of labour develops, there is no guarantee that it would benefit the same developing countries as those from which large numbers of migrants come at present. For much of the new industry, at least in the early years, would probably grow up in the richer developing countries, which already have more expertise in production and marketing.

Many people think of modern migration as the supply of labour for the rich white countries. But the labour importing countries now include, as well as Europe, the United States and South Africa, a number of the oil states. Travelling in the developing countries, I kept hearing stories of the actual or potential labour demands of Iran, Saudi Arabia and the Gulf States. Many of the poorer countries see this as a great new opportunity to alleviate their unemployment. One estimate is that the Middle East will require 2 million skilled workers over the next five years.

There may be great disappointments ahead. The scope for development in the newly rich OPEC states is enormous. But the pace of development may be slowed by the gross inequities of wealth, and therefore the number of workers needed may be less than many expect. Will it be enough to make any significant impact on Asian and African levels of unemployment and underemployment? As one migration expert said, 'If the Shah does ask for 700,000 Indians, that's only a drop in their bucket.' Yet already three-quarters of Kuwait's labour force is foreign in origin, as is two-fifths of Saudi Arabia's and one-third of Bahrain's.

It will be interesting to see whether the OPEC countries, with their special links in the Third World, will be more willing than the advanced nations have been to allow countries which supply them with labour to select who should go. The developing countries would like to use migration more effectively to alleviate their domestic problems. It would help, for example, if they could encourage migration by people, particularly those from agricultural districts and from depressed areas, who have not enough work at home and who would benefit from training abroad.

Suggestions are being made that incentives for such migrants to return when they have been trained would help to build up a skilled work force.

There is also a strong feeling that financial opportunities are being missed. Although remittances sent by migrants to their relatives, often at considerable sacrifice, contribute much to personal well-being, governments are being urged to organise savings societies and co-operatives in order to channel some of the overseas money into productive invest-ment. One ILO official also has a vision of extracting from the industrial countries dormant social security funds of about 2000 million dollars, which he estimates are due to returning immigrants, and using them for investment.

The brain drain is a separate but similar problem. The figures here are startling: during the sixties, about a quarter of a million highly skilled and professional people migrated to North America, Western Europe and Australia. To take a few examples from this global total, about one-third of the United States intake consisted of Indian scientists and engineers and Filipino scientists, engineers and physicians. The effects on the exporting countries were serious: the Philippines lost about half of the nurses who graduated in 1970, and even higher proportions of physicians, surgeons and dentists. The benefits to the United States were considerable, for the migrants provided between a quarter and a half of the country's increase in physicians and surgeons, between 15 and 25 per cent of the increase in engineers, and one in ten of the new scientists.

Two principal proposals have been made on how the developing countries can be protected from the hardship this causes. One is to impose a bonding scheme on graduates, so that if they want to emigrate they must repay the cost of their subsidised education to their own country. The other is that the receiving country should impose a special im-migrant's income tax and remit the revenue to the exporting country.

Such schemes might be difficult to launch, but not as difficult as the more fundamental cure being proposed by the ILO for migration and the underdevelopment which causes it. This is the adoption in industrial countries of adequate development policies. The argument here runs into a strange limbo between free market economics and the planned economy. But do not be misled by labels, for people change sides with bewildering speed. If there were no national limitations on the movement of capital or of trade, doubtless many older industries in the developed world would have gone where the labour was cheapest and most amenable. Instead they have stayed where the markets are, because they could not face a tariff wall between them and their customers.

Advocates of adjustment policies believe in freer trade, but they accept the political reality: that this will not come about unless the livelihoods of displaced workers are adequately safeguarded. Since many of them combine faith in freer trade with belief in a high degree of national economic planning, they find no difficulty in advocating the most elaborate adjustment schemes in rich countries.

I must admit to a feeling that adjustment policies in Western countries sound like an excellent economic theory, but that in practice they are unlikely to happen with such crisp efficiency. But before examining the difficulties, let us first understand the theory. In simple terms, it is this: as freer trade in manufactured goods and processed foodstuffs allowed developing countries to increase their exports, and therefore their incomes, they would be able to buy more goods from the West. This would enable the more sophisticated Western manufacturing industries to expand, with the workers who had been displaced in the declining, labour-intensive industries finding new and more lucrative jobs in modern occupations. Thus, there would be more and better jobs in both rich and poor countries.

The experts take care to acknowledge that this cannot happen overnight. They are aware of the trade union scepticism about adjustment assistance, which is derisively known as 'burial grant'. The unions' suspicion derives from their historic experience *within* their own countries, where employers used the existence of masses of unorganised and desperately poor people to undermine the growing power of the unions. If they let down their defences, will the same use not be made of the very poor of the developing countries, whose numbers are so much greater?

As a result of this reasoning, the unions, while remaining among the strongest advocates in many advanced countries of more generous aid, are opponents of free trade policies, which involve the import of competing goods. They are also extremely suspicious of a new international division of labour, and would prefer to talk about an 'international expansion of employment everywhere'.

But critics of the unions argue that they are foolish to persuade governments to cling on to industries which are doomed in the long run anyhow. Much better to use government subsidies to create new industries, while re-training workers, helping them to move where they need to, and maintaining their incomes during the transitional period.

A major obstacle to such policies is that the men and women who are displaced by structural change in industry are often disadvantaged in one way or another — by age, sex, the depressed area they live in, the long decline in their industry, the difficulty of acquiring the right skills, and so on. One of the classical examples given of how the advanced countries might redeploy their labour is by moving out of textiles and into the manufacture of textile machinery, which would then be used by developing countries. But many of the workers displaced would be middle-aged women, with little chance of a new career in engineering, certainly, and less chance than most of a new start even in other light industries. Textiles, indeed, is a good example of a traditional and somewhat conservative industry which has found it par-ticularly hard to adapt to a changed world. A former Lancashire cotton worker said recently: 'We were always told that nobody in the world could weave like us. We ought to have known that was wrong, of course, because if I could learn the essentials of the trade in a few weeks, why not someone in a developing country? But it still came as a shock.'

To a politician or an official in the Third World, or to an international expert, contemplating the infinite poverty he is attempting to alleviate, the problems of workers in rich countries often seem merely a feeble excuse by governments for their inaction. Like many of the contrasts in this story, the plight of a Lancashire cotton worker and of an Indian peasant who might not get a job in a cotton mill are different in kind: one, at worst, could fall back on the allowances paid by a welfare state; the other might die during the next famine. But then, many of the contrasts are obscene: to eat a square meal in Dacca or Calcutta seems pitifully out of tune with what exists outside the hotel. If we are talking about what is politically feasible, we ought to face the practical and psychological difficulty about adjustment in the richer countries: the burden of change tends to fall on their least fortunate people.

It has been estimated that if all the trade restrictions were removed at a stroke, somewhere between 2.5 and 3.5 million workers in industrialised countries would have to find new jobs. But since only a small number of developing countries would be able to take advantage of the export opportunities, nothing so cataclysmic for the world economy is possible. A transition period of between ten and twenty years would be inevitable, and the total number of people affected in developed countries by any conceivable move to free trade during that time would be about 1 million. So over the transition period, the task would be to find work for about 70,000 to 100,000 each year.

The ILO argues that this is not unmanageable, and objectively this is so. But will developed nations, many of them depressed by their most traumatic economic setback in forty years, achieve the dynamism which is acknowledged to be essential for successful adjustment policies? Everyone pays lip service to the belief that firms and workers affected by imports to developed countries must not be left to bear the burden of change on their own, while their neighbours benefit from cheaper goods (if they are actually sold more cheaply in the shops, that is). But the reason adjustment programmes have had limited success in all but a few developed countries is that the atmosphere is wrong. Educational, social, and active manpower policies which create an upwardly mobile labour force are essential, as well as economic policies that encourage innovative and competitive production of new lines. Without that spirit in favour of change, subsidies for individual projects cannot produce enough overall dynamism in the economy to help those who are hurt by change.

It has been estimated that it would cost between $300 million and $500 million a year to fund an adjustment programme on the scale necessary. However, the ILO argues that the United States alone is at present $10,000 *million* annually worse off than it need be, because of protection on the products likely to be involved in trade with developing countries. It warns of the sad fates which have overtaken countries that have failed to move with the times, and argues that there is no better investment for the rich nations than in the restructuring of their economies. If the poor countries will only also agree to follow a basic needs strategy, which will benefit all their people, as well as opening up new markets, the whole world would be on the road to growth and higher living standards.

That is the vision of the development specialists. What is likely to happen? It is all too probable that the rich countries will remain more rather than less self-centered; less rather than more dynamic in structural change; putting their own anxiety, at a time of hardship throughout the world, ahead of the interests of the world's poor. Just as, within the Third World, the rich will probably put their own interests ahead of those of the poor.

That is what is likely to happen. Yet all logic ought to tell us that we will benefit from the more courageous, more radical course of change based on mutual interest. It would be instructive for both idealists and sceptics to look briefly at the one group in the world which is promoting, in a practical way, a new international division of labour — the multi-national companies. To many people, they are the new devils — in the Third World, devils of neo-colonialism; among workers in the developed world, devils of self-serving capitalism. There they go, seeking profit at any cost, bribing politicians, subverting governments, exploiting cheap labour, extracting expensive tax concessions from poor nations, refusing to recognise trade unions, throwing workers on the scrapheap.

All these, and many other allegations, are true in some places and at some times. Because of them, the International Confederation of Free Trade Unions would like an international agency to supervise the companies' activities.

Without such an agency, they say, the multinationals will blackmail the poor countries, disrupt the economies of the richer ones, export pollution, and ignore trade union rights, the health and job security of workers, and the national sovereignty and economic independence of whole peoples. They will use 'slippery, if not strictly illegal, financial practices' to evade taxes, and they will switch their money around the world at the stroke of a telephone, causing chaos in the international monetary system.

That represents the views of many workers in industrialised countries. Even from the Third World's point of view, there is much wrong with multinationals. They are, for example, failing to provide as many jobs as the governments which encouraged them expected. The total, from a huge investment, is only about 2 million jobs, 0.3 per cent of the labour force in the developing countries. Often the multinationals tilt technology in a direction which is against the long-term interests of the people — in favour of capital, and against the more liberal employment of labour. They have failed to do as much as they could to encourage local enterprise by sub-contracting. And they have not done as much research into appropriate technology as their resources would so easily allow.

Yet for all their limitations, in some cases their wickednesses, the multinationals have been a unique instrument for bringing capital, entrepreneurship and technical knowledge to countries which would not have got them in any other way. They have not only imported capital; they have financed three-quarters of their investment out of retained earnings or local savings mobilised in the capital market. In fact, they have brought to the Third World not only production skills, but also knowledge of how to organise finance, raw materials, transport and marketing.

Like most human institutions, the multinationals are a mixture of good and bad. But their value is shown by their presence, usually by invitation, in many Third World countries, and more recently in Communist countries also. Often they have been allowed to drive too hard a bargain, financially and in other ways. This has sometimes been because of a corrupt relationship between them and leading people in the administration of the host country. In future, the Third World needs to organise itself to drive harder bargains, designed to benefit ordinary people.

Yet in a world where progress towards development and the elimination of poverty is painfully slow, it is hard to argue against the multinationals, for all their faults. What workers in both developing and developed nations need is a better balance of power between themselves and these international giants. That means stronger and better organised unions. It does not mean throttling the multinationals before an alternative means of doing the same jobs has been created.

10 The World's Chance to Change

Trade and aid are two points at which two worlds meet: the relatively affluent world of the industrialised, market economy countries, suffering from recession now, certainly, and with their own pockets of unemployment, underemployment and poverty; and the Third World, with its pockets of affluence, certainly, particularly in the oil exporting nations and in a dozen or so others which are on their way to becoming industrialised, yet with a great impoverished mass of people to whom at present no hope of a better life is offered.

The market economies and the Third World: it is ironic that although the global debate on development often flirts with either one or the other of the principal economic ideologies, socialism and capitalism, the Communist countries come into the real argument only as an ideological gadfly. For the proportions of either trade or aid they are concerned with are so small that they cannot significantly affect the outcome. The poor countries do 5 per cent of their trade with the Communist bloc, 20 per cent with each other, and the remaining 75 per cent with the market economies of the West. The West also contributes about 75 per cent of aid, and the OPEC countries have now far surpassed the Communists for the second place.

Of these two subjects, trade and aid, it is fashionable now to say that trade is more important. For the national self-esteem of the developing countries and for their long-term economic development, that is certainly true. In the fifteen years between 1955 and 1970, the developing countries' share of world trade fell by an amount which was statistically equivalent to 72 million additional jobs. That is how much trade matters.

Yet we ought not to under-rate the significance, particularly in the short term, of aid. Perhaps we ought to think of what is called development assistance as *first* aid. For if we accept that this generation in the Third World cannot be saved from want, and even starvation by a rapid development of modern industry, but must rely on a basic needs strategy concentrated on the rural areas where the vast majority of poorest people live, then aid is crucial. One of the tragedies of the seventies is the rich world's failure to maintain its good intentions on aid. Just as development experts were learning how to use it more sensibly — by directing it to the poor, through labour-intensive projects in agriculture, irrigation, water supplies, sewerage, rural roads, and everything which will develop the life of the countryside — the amounts have declined.

Partly this is economics. With two recessions in the past decade, the present one deeper and harsher than a post-Keynesian generation had thought possible, the developed countries were bound to feel poor, and to react accordingly. But the difficulty in extracting more aid from the richer countries is also, in part, psychological.

The truth is that the West, and particularly the United States, feels itself driven into a corner. One cause is the rhetorical aggression of the Third World, itself a result of exasperation. America, whose own riches are based on a system of private enterprise, hears itself engulfed in a sea of socialist jargon. It must not make it any easier to bear that some of those mouthing it are Third World élitists whose genuine dedication to any egalitarian philosophy is suspect. Add the threat that many of the developing countries will slip into the diplomatic sphere of influence of the Soviet Union or China — probably not a real threat, but a worry none the less — and you have a recipe for mutual distrust.

Some in the West feel their ideology strongly also. At the United Nations recently, the West German Foreign Minister, Hans-Dietrich Genscher, attributed his country's remarkable recovery after the Second World War to the decision then taken in favour of a free market economy, and he gave a warning against paralysing the efficiency of the world by 'dirigistic experiments'. The task of reform in the international system, he argued, must be to preserve the efficiency of the market, but at the same time to link it with effective help for the weak.

That, Europeans maintain, is what their Economic Community did in the Lomé Convention with the forty-six African, Caribbean and Pacific states: the European Nine created 'a unilateral free trade area' to help countries whose level of development was so far behind their own that the working of the market did not provide an adequate way to help them. It was not a coincidence that the most doughty opponents of the developing countries' demands for a New International Economic Order at the Seventh Special Session of the UN in New York in September 1975 were Germany, Japan and the United States, countries which have seen their own prosperity grow, rapidly and recently, through international trade on a comparatively free market.

The Americans suffer most obviously from Third World attacks. They have felt diplomatically on the defensive since their withdrawal from Indo-China, and the rapid transformation of their former natural majority in the UN bodies into an equally automatic majority of the Third World and the Communists has done nothing for the shortness of American tempers. The outburst by the US Ambassador to the UN, Daniel Moynihan, on the occasion of President Amin's unctuous speech as President of the Organisation of African Unity, ought not to be ignored. Mr Moynihan spoke for many in his own and other countries when he refused to be lectured by a racialist spokesman for an area where democratic government has been in rapid retreat. If the rich and poor worlds are to live together in reasonable generosity of spirit, they will have to find means to tolerate each other's preconceptions on political and economic principles, rather as the Communists and the West have gradually done.

So much for the background to the West's failure to provide enough aid. What are the facts? It seems probable that during the seventies, the poorest 1000 million people in the Third World will make no progress at all in their living standards, and that both they and the 725 million people in the developing countries who are less poor will fall further behind the 675 million people in the industrial countries.

The rich world set out on this decade with the intention of contributing in aid 0.7 per cent of its gross national product. At present, the average from these countries is only 0.33 per cent, and it has been estimated that, on present trends, by 1980 that will fall back further to 0.28 per cent. The result of this and of the world recession is frightening. The poorest 1000 million people, with a per capita income of less than $200, now have declining incomes. The best that can be expected is that the average income of these people will grow over the whole ten years from 1970 to 1980 by a miserable $3. What a decade of hope! Yet the average man in the rich world can hope to be $900 richer over that period.

Partly, of course, it has all gone wrong because the world economy has moved from a period of optimism to one of bewilderment. The fifties and sixties produced high growth in the industrial countries, and with it a hopefulness which begat generosity. But since then the international monetary system has run into trouble, energy supply has been made a nightmare by the oil embargoes and price increases, anxiety about the environment and the exhaustion of natural resources has caused people to doubt what their futures will be, the West has become more sensitive about the social and political perils of the pockets of poverty amid its affluence, and the massive importation of cheap labour — although, as has been seen, it is part of the problem of Third World poverty — is perceived as a new cause of social stress. All these factors have made the rich countries more introspective and less willing to help the poorer nations.

Even before recession set in seriously, the rot in our generosity had set in. In real terms, this has been a more rapidly growing neglect than most of us in the West realise. The ILO has calculated that, allowing for inflation and currency realignments, aid has decreased by about 7 per cent in the ten years to 1973. Governments and legislatures in the rich countries, though sensitive enough to the effects of inflation at home, seem oblivious of how it erodes the value of their aid. Yet this cut of 7 per cent in real aid happened in a decade when people's real incomes in the industrial countries rose by nearly half.

There are some bright spots. The oil exporting countries now seem to be taking on greater responsibilities for aid as they see the misery which has flowed from the events of 1973. They were paying about 3 per cent of their GNP in aid during 1975. This, of course, was only one-tenth of their staggering balance of payments surpluses, but it still represented about one-sixth of the world's aid to the developing countries. There were warnings, however, that the oil states could not be expected to keep up such a high level of aid, because their trade balances were diminishing as the world curbed its appetite for the more expensive oil. The aid was also described as 'still highly concentrated', which is a polite way of saying that Moslem is helping Moslem.

We have learned a lot in recent years about how aid ought to be distributed (ideally, that is if none of the donor nations had trade interests, or senses of obligation to former colonies, or ideological hang-ups of one kind or another). The Third World, the phrase used in this book to describe all the developing countries, is now being sub-divided into the Third and Fourth Worlds. The former title is used for those nations which, although they are still developing, have a lot on their side compared with the really poor. Apart from the major oil countries, these include fifteen others among the 152 nations which are generally classed as developing. These fifteen among them account for nine-tenths of the Third World's manufactured exports and for most of the acceleration in growth. They are Argentina, Brazil, Mexico, Puerto Rico, Guinea, Zambia, Cyprus, Israel, Syria, Malaysia, Pakistan, Korea, Hong Kong, Singapore and Taiwan.

It is the residue of the poor countries, the Fourth World, which desperately needs more aid. It contains three-quarters of the population of the developing countries, and has a per capita income of $135. Most of the population works in subsistence agriculture. These countries' exports are almost entirely from their agricultural sectors, and these have been declining sharply as a proportion of world trade. Yet as their populations grow, they need to import more food.

The flow of private capital, which is the best hope of rapid growth for some of the fifteen countries listed above, does not go to these really poor nations, for their economies are not far enough advanced to give much scope for industrial investment: the infrastructure, education, administration, even the systems of effective security and justice are often not good enough to attract businessmen from abroad.

This is why the international aid organisations are now tilting their assistance heavily towards the poorest nations, towards agriculture, and towards the urban poor. Donor nations are being advised that they can help most if they pay local and recurrent costs, such as wages, instead of just concentrating, as too often in the past, on providing expensive and not wholly suitable capital equipment — or, as it was once somewhat tactlessly put, the donor nations' own 'inefficiently produced and overpriced exports'.

As well as fulfilling the human instinct to be most charitable to the most desperately poor, this advice re-presents good economics. If ways can be found to raise the productivity and therefore the incomes of poor peasants, they will not only be more capable of feeding themselves, but their marketable surpluses of agricultural goods will increase. And that, in most countries of the developing world, remains the best hope of raising large sums of money for investment, even eventually in the manufacturing sector. This change in the direction in which aid is going ought to do something to stop the growing inequality *within* the poor world, though as long as the absolute amount of aid available remains stagnant, the countries which had got their development plans off the ground before the crisis of the seventies will enjoy a great advantage.

Some of the aid donors were beginning to give advice as well as getting it. Into their vocabulary, though gently, there crept a hint of the trade-off between national and inter-national policies which has been a recurring theme in this book. For example, John Grant, one of the British ministers responsible for aid, commented in *The Times* on the 1975 report of the World Bank:

> The report is critical of the way some developing countries provide a level of service for the middle classes well above anything they do for their poor people. It is a thoroughly justified criticism. There is much to be done, too, by

genuine income redistribution and land reform. These are actions for the developing nations, and although we cannot and should not set fixed conditions for our aid which may impinge on local political decision-making and smack of neo-colonialism, it is logical that our poverty-oriented programmes should take these factors into account as we apply it, although getting our policy messages through to recipient governments is an inevitably lengthy and sometimes delicate process.

That was written for Mr Grant's British readers. In fairness, it is a message which ought to be given, without equivocation, by the British and other governments at the ILO's conference. It is only fair to the governments of the Third World to make clear that the West is worried that its aid is not reaching enough of the world's most desperately poor people. And it is only fair to those people, whose own political influence is practically non-existent, to put pressure on their governments to set their own houses in order and begin a radical policy of domestic reform, including income redistribution and land reform. But the West will only have the influence to do this if its aid is increased again to levels of which it can be proud. The trade-off, in fact, has a kind of rough moral justice in it.

But what about trade? Development aid transfers about $14, 500 million from rich to poor countries. The exports of the developing countries bring in something over $100,000 million. The Third World believes that a sharp increase in this latter figure is what will produce a real economic leap forward. How can it be done?

This is the worst conceivable time to ask the question. As I write, the recession is at what we hope is its lowest point. The markets of the industrialised world have not been so depressed since well before the Second World War. Looking at overall statistics, one might be excused for thinking that the developing countries have not done so badly out of this as might have been expected. For while the share of developing countries in world trade has fallen steadily throughout the sixties — from 21 per cent in 1960 to 18 per cent in 1970 — and remained there for the three following years, there was a dramatic increase in the market share, to

27 per cent, in 1974.

Alas, the huge increase in oil prices at the end of 1973 was almost wholly responsible for this. In fact, the total oil revenue of the eleven major exporting countries in 1974 was nearly as much as the total export earnings of the whole Third World had been the previous year. That was the measure of the killing the oil states made through their cartel.

Meanwhile, however, the poor countries which did not possess any oil were savagely hit. Their own oil bills went up sharply, the recession in the rich countries reduced their markets, and they were also affected by a fall in commodity prices. The theory that the cartel arrangements, which had been so successful for oil, could be used for other commodities also, quickly evaporated after the producers of copper had tried and failed. A world in recession does not favour the sellers of anything; it was another lesson in how interdependent we are. The indirect effects of the oil troubles have been mentioned earlier. A Rockefeller Foundation expert has estimated that as many as 20 million people may die because of crop shortages caused primarily by lack of fertiliser as a result of the oil crisis.

As we turn from aid to trade, commodity prices ought to come next in the league table of what is most important to the poorest people in the world. But more heat is generated over manufactured goods, and particularly over the tariff and non-tariff barriers to their importation from developing countries, for both sides in this dispute are articulate, and perhaps the issues are easier to understand. For the future development of countries which have already established their industrial bases, freer trade in manufactures is vital, and it will eventually grow in importance for everyone, as each of the poor countries in turn pushes its way towards a modern economy. But in the immediate future, the problem of commodity prices is more significant to more people than is manufacturing. The problem of commodities is this: about twenty-five of the least developed countries in the world rely on one or two commodities for the bulk of their export earnings. If the markets for these crops diminish, or if the price collapses, their economies suffer terribly. There is great conflict over even what *has* happened to commodity prices in recent years, much more over what *ought* to happen. In particular, there is dispute over what quantity of commodities a developing country has to export in order to import the quantity of manufactures that the same money would buy from the industrialised countries five, ten or twenty years ago.

A team of economists, assembled by UNCTAD, could not find any clear evidence of a long-term deterioration in the net barter terms of trade of developing countries, though they noted substantial fluctuations over shorter periods. But two of their number, operating on different economic criteria, believed that the terms of trade had been moving against the developing countries, and the UNCTAD office itself estimated that the value of commodities against manufactures had fallen by an average of about 2 per cent annually over a twenty-year period.

There is some freely acknowledged gamesmanship here: different people select different dates in order to prove different cases. What is not in dispute is that if the poorest developing countries are to make steady progress towards alleviating their worst poverty, they would need more assured markets, and better prices, for their commodities, in addition to the diversification of their own agriculture and of their economies generally. But when it comes to methods, again there is a dispute.

What the developing countries would like is an index linking commodity prices to those of manufacturers. The United States and the Western European countries acknowledge the need to stabilise the prices of raw materials, but all of them are opposed to an index. One of the snags raised is that poor countries produce only about a quarter of the world's trade in commodities, so that an index would also benefit the agriculturists of some of the richest countries, notably the United States, Canada and Australia, who would stand to gain on their grain and other food exports.

Sometimes the argument presents itself as one of ideology, between a Third World arguing for 'managed' markets and the developed countries convinced that everyone benefits if the markets are free. But like most ideological confrontations, this is an over-simplification of the respective positions. At the Seventh Special Session of the UN General Assembly, the leadership of the developing countries seemed to be passing from those who were determined on some kind of victory on principle, to those who favoured getting the best practical deal they could in a world whose economic climate had dramatically deteriorated since their New International Economic Order had been formulated.

On the Western side, the commitment to free market ideology was not total either. It was generally acknowledged that some kind of international commodity agreements were needed, and that there must be a rising trend in prices for the Third World's goods. It was a belief that the West was ready to make a deal which softened attitudes in the developing countries' delegations in New York. But the anxieties of the advocates of the market economy were expressed, on this issue also, by Hans-Dietrich Genscher, of West Germany.

He warned the developing countries that they would be wise to ensure that their prices rise in line with developments in supply and demand. Artificially high prices would not be worthwhile for producers if they resulted in slackening demand, replacement by substitute products, and the appearance in the market of new producers, often from industrial countries. He argued that the outcome for the original producers in the poor countries would be falling, instead of rising export earnings, and for the world's economy as a whole a transition from low-cost to high-cost production.

The German view was that developing countries' export earnings should be increased not by administered prices, but via the workings of the market — in other words, by increasing productivity and hence profits, by boosting sales, by entering the initial processing stages. That last proposal, in particular, rang hollow in many Third World ears, for as soon as the producer countries begin processing their raw materials, they run into various tariff and other barriers to trade. But more of that later.

Attitudes are changing, even if not so quickly as many people would like. In Europe, particularly since the oil crisis, there has been growing awareness of how much the continent relies on the developing countries. Europe imports 95 per cent of its energy needs, 75 per cent of its raw materials for steel making, 65 per cent of its copper, 57 per cent of its bauxite, 99 per cent of its phosphates, nearly all its cobalt, 86 per cent of its tin ore, all of its manganese, 95 per cent of its tungsten, 92 per cent of its coffee, and all of its cocoa and oil seeds.

M. Claude Cheysson, of the European Economic Commission, put the issue bluntly:

> The world economic order was built by the industrialised powers for themselves. It was indifferent to others . . . We in Europe had to work less and less to acquire a certain amount of minerals, wood or groundnuts, but found it legitimate, without thinking about it very clearly, that the suppliers of our raw materials should work more and more to buy the same tractor or power station. We are beginning to understand that these producers of raw materials want to develop and not simply survive.

Yet, whatever happened over the previous twenty years, the terms of world trade certainly have moved against the developing countries since the oil crisis. Although the prices of their exports rose by 27 per cent during 1974, for example, the cost of their imports went up by 40 per cent. And deepening world recession cut the volume of their exports.

The most alarming estimate of the increase in the developing countries' oil import bill was that it would use up nearly all their foreign aid. Another measure of the effect on individual countries was to set the size of the increase in the cost of their oil against their total export earnings: 30 per cent for Ethiopia and India, 25 per cent for Brazil, Korea and Thailand, 20 per cent for Bangladesh and Pakistan.

To complete the staggering story of the cost of the oil-induced recession, it is necessary to look at the debt figures. The trade deficits of the non-oil developing countries leaped from $9000 million in 1973 to an estimated $36,000 million in 1975. Their accumulated foreign debts had risen to $120,000 million, which meant that half of all new assistance would have to be used for interest payments. The Indian Foreign Minister, Y.B. Chavan, whose country has had to borrow even for consumption, told the United Nations that unless India got further concessional transfers of money, most of its aid would go on interest on debts.

Faced with such figures, some people argued that there was a case for simply cancelling the debts of the poorest countries. Others argued that it would be hard to discriminate between countries, that debt cancellation removes all financial discipline for the future, and that instead a way must be found of funding debts over a longer period. Britain announced to the Special Assembly that it would give aid in outright grants, instead of loans, in future. Sometime soon there is going to be an international conference to devise means to lighten this appalling burden of debt.

That was one difficult subject at the Special Assembly. But the commodities problem, from which we digressed, proved just as difficult. The rich world maintained its resistance to indexation. But it knew that commodity prices were an explosive subject; if any evidence of that were needed, oil provided it, for the producers of that remarkable commodity had taken the law into their own hands, with disastrous consequences for the world. So the rich countries at least acknowledged their own need for reliable supplies of commodities at reliable prices, and they realised that in return for that, they must concede case by case studies of the commodity markets, leading to a system which would protect the export earnings of developing countries. It was only a beginning, but it was a good beginning.

Commodities claim much attention, because they are an important element in a basic needs strategy, which is increasingly seen as the best means of development for many countries. But however strong the intellectual case for such a strategy may be, many developing countries themselves remain obsessed with industrial development as an engine of growth. Emulation of the West dies hard.

The developing countries contain 70 per cent of the world's population, but at present they contribute only 7 per cent of its industrial production. Their aim is to have at least a quarter of the world's industrial capacity by the end of the century. Many politicians and officials in the Third World know that the development of agriculture and progress in the informal urban sector are more likely to produce better living conditions quickly for a mass of their fellow countrymen. But they retain a fear that they will be left as the hewers of wood and drawers of water in a world in which the clever — and profitable — work will be done by the rich countries. Their perception of what has happened in the commodities markets over the years confirms that fear. For better or worse, the struggle to get new industries to developing countries will continue. It must only be hoped that it will not obstruct policies which might bring more immediate relief to the poorest.

It is doubtful whether the industrialisation drive is being conducted as well as it might be. It often seems that the developing countries get the worst of both worlds by their naive or ambivalent treatment of multinational companies. As was mentioned in an earlier chapter, this is sometimes because there is too cosy a relationship, often of a corrupt or semi-corrupt financial nature, between the politicians or officials of the host country and the multinational. But on other occasions, it is simply because the host country is so anxious to have the extra employment and the technical know-how of the multinational, that it is prepared to sell its facilities too cheaply.

At the opposite extreme, some of the rhetoric of the New International Economic Order must frighten off multinationals, which are, after all, one of the more uncompromising exponents of capitalism in a world in which that system tends to be politically on the defensive. In its public declarations, the Third World speaks the language of socialism. Sometimes, as in the case of Tanzania, this is entirely appropriate, for the practice matches the precept. But is it really so appropriate to India, or Kenya, or many other developing countries in which the bastions of privilege tower a good deal higher above the heads of the common people than they do in the social democracies of the West?

Yet the words that emerge from the Non-Aligned Group, the UN International Development Organisation, and other bodies in which the developing countries are dominant must curdle the blood in many a boardroom where investment is being considered. Take this, for example, from the UN's

Charter of Economic Rights and Duties of States:

> Each state has the right to nationalise, expropriate, or transfer ownership of foreign property, in which case appropriate compensation should be paid by the state adopting such measures, taking into account its relevant laws and regulations and all circumstances that the state considers pertinent. In any case where the question of compensation gives rise to a controversy, it shall be settled under the domestic law of the nationalising state, and by its tribunals, unless it is freely and mutually agreed by all states concerned that other peaceful means be sought on the basis of the sovereign equality of states and in accordance with the principles of free choice of means.

The activities of companies like ITT in Chile make such declarations eminently understandable. The developing countries feel they owe it to their own self-respect to assert their sovereignty over what they regard — in some cases, justifiably — as a perpetuation by the industries of the rich world of something suspiciously like the old colonial system. But the danger is that mere rhetoric will frighten away capital, without actually achieving much. In one of the documents emerging from the Third World on this subject, the nationalisation of foreign assets is called 'that inalienable right'. Again, the assertion of the right is for understandable reasons: the invasion of Suez, after all, is still only twenty years away, and many leaders of developing countries are still suspicious of the armed might of the West.

The difficulty about talking so much about nationalisation and expropriation, however, is that enough of the world still exists as a free market to give industrialists 'an inalienable right' also: only to invest their money where they think it will be safe. Their attitudes are very much in the melting-pot at present. At the time of the Seventh Special Session in New York, a senior official of the Chase Manhattan Bank spoke about the deteriorating relationship between some Third World governments and the multinationals, and said he was pessimistic about the likelihood that private capital flows would meet the needs of the poor nations.

The sad and futile fact is that the damaging rhetoric and

the reality are often far apart. One executive of a multi-national company, who has great experience of negotiating with Third World governments, wryly comments that there is a startling difference between what they say in public about foreign capital and what they say in private. An international official confirms that such ambiguity is widespread: 'All that rhetoric about the wicked capitalists, even the New Inter-national Economic Order itself, is a tactic to divert attention from their internal difficulties. It doesn't achieve much, but they reckon it buys them a breathing space.' The question is: how much does the breathing space cost?

The developing countries' growing interest in freer trade in manufactures comes at a time when the world's trading system is already in transition, not to say chaos. The breakdown of the old international monetary system is part of the story. The growth of the European Economic Community into an area which includes almost all the significant economies of Western Europe is another. At the same time, the conviction is growing that tariffs are an ineffective protection: particularly in labour-intensive indus-tries like textiles, clothing and footwear, the comparative advantage of the developing countries has grown too large to be frustrated by tariffs at any politically acceptable level. Add to this the determination of multinational companies (with the political reservations mentioned above) to fight their way over, through or round tariff barriers, to use the Trojan horse of investment to flatten the tariff wall if necessary, and one begins to understand why Western governments are coming to regard tariffs with distaste or boredom.

In the Tokyo round of trade negotiations, which will not really begin to make progress until the world emerges from its recession, the most radical suggestion is that the industrial countries should agree on a complete elimination of tariffs and of all except temporary non-tariff restrictions on trade in industrial products over ten or twenty years. Those who advocate this approach have a good psychological argument. So long as uncertainty remains, they say, those industries in advanced countries which face competition from the Third World will devote all their political skill and effort, both on the manufacturers' and trade union sides, to force their governments to maintain protection of one kind or another. But once a firm international plan to lower barriers has been agreed upon, the same effort would be devoted to adjustment policies, aimed at finding scope for investment and employment in occupations where the rich countries still enjoy a comparative advantage.

One of the barriers which ought to be lowered is GATT's Article 19. Although this was intended to allow countries to take 'emergency' action where one of their industries is in real difficulty, it has often turned into a new and semi-permanent protection. One proposal is that in future such 'temporary' arrangements should have a definite time-scale, that they should be open to international supervision, and that the government taking the emergency action should also begin adjustment measures to move the workers concerned into more suitable employment.

The staff at GATT have counted more than 800 non-tariff devices to restrict imports. The most obvious are the 'buy American', 'buy British', 'buy French' campaigns into which many countries are pushed from time to time. It has been estimated that between $30,000 million and $40,000 million worth of goods are protected by such campaigns. Most of that protection, of course, is against the products of other rich countries, but the Third World also feels the side-effects.

One of the most common restrictions now affecting Third World exporting countries is the so-called 'voluntary' agreement, made on a bilateral basis, for the exporting government to limit the amounts sent to a particular market. It sometimes seems that the importing government makes the exporting Third World country the offer of a voluntary deal it cannot refuse (to borrow a happy phrase from the Mafia). For in the background, there is always a threat that import quotas may be used.

Yet all these restrictions look like sand-castles standing in the way of the tide. The industrial and social pattern of the rich countries, for a variety of reasons, is changing. In Western Europe, for example, the period of unrestricted immigration is probably ending. More and more, both multinationals and national companies which try to compete with them in the areas where the migrants have been employed, including iron and steel production and chemicals as well as the more traditional labour-intensive industries, will have to think about their future. Many may decide, provided the political difficulties are not too daunting, that they can best avoid being overwhelmed by labour, environmental and other problems by investing in the developing countries.

What would give this movement a real stimulus is the expectation of growing markets in the Third World. How quickly will development go, how soon will spending power filter down from the comparatively small numbers who buy consumer goods now to the great masses of the population? Can the poor countries get on to a development path which benefits hundreds of millions of their people, rather than just a few millions? Such questions are important to the Western businessman, considering his investment decisions, just as they are important, at a more life and death level, to the peasant on the verge of starvation in Asia, Africa or Latin America.

One way of assisting a break-through would be to increase trade *within* the Third World. Despite the huge increases in populations, such trade now represents only 3.5 per cent of world trade, compared with nearly 5 per cent in 1960. There are many reasons for this disappointing trend. The large markets of the former metropolitan countries have usually seemed the more attractive to newly independent nations. For one thing, they are familiar: finance, marketing, transport and communications have always been pointed in that direction. But the developing nations are beginning to recognise the great opportunity for self-generating growth and for economies of scale if they can increasingly learn to provide for each other's needs. The large amounts of money which some of the oil states now have available to spend ought to confirm this tendency.

There are other actions which developing countries can take: break down their own constraints on the supply side, improve their market research, sales promotion, product design and quality. But if one examines such issues in detail, two connected facts emerge. One is that, despite Third World wariness about foreign capital, the type of package of capital, technology and managerial expertise which an international group — whether a multinational company or a bank — can offer is often the best hope of a quick break-through into international markets for manufactures on a large scale.

But the second fact is that such private capital will inevitably flow to the relatively advanced among the developing countries, for that is where the infrastructure makes rapid industrial growth possible. Between two-thirds and four-fifths of private capital in this area already goes to such countries, which contain only one-quarter of the population of the Third World. So most of the new jobs which private maufacturing industry creates are going to be in the better off among the poor countries, those which are already on the threshhold of sustained industrial growth.

That brings us back to where this chapter began: aid. Unless the flow of aid to the poor countries revives, a new inequality is going to be created and extended — that between the Third World countries which 'have arrived', and those which struggle on in a new Fourth World of financial chaos, underdevelopment and poverty.

Since the emphasis in this book has been on what can be done by developing countries and by the international community to promote development at the most basic level, in agriculture and the informal trades of the cities, it is right to record an alternative, or perhaps a complementary, optimism. Those who put more emphasis on freer trade are optimistic about what can be achieved if the liberal policies of the post-war period are continued until the end of the century. One estimate exceeds the Third World target: they would have two-thirds of the quantity of industrial production that the rich countries have in the year 2000. But this estimate depends on investment really being allowed to follow comparative advantage, as water runs downhill, and without any of the dams of trade restriction.

Jan Tumlir, of GATT, who made the estimate, maintains that workers in the developed countries ought not to worry: so long as the problem is set against a perspective of about thirty years, the rich world can achieve very high rates of import absorption, without any displacement or transfer of workers who are at present employed in vulnerable industries:

All that is necessary is for those industries to reduce their rate of hiring, and for the public authorities to provide educational and vocational training systems which can qualify the new entrants into the labour force for employment in the high-wage and dynamic industries whose expansion is already being inhibited by short supply of adequately skilled labour.

Tumlir argues that extreme protectionists in the West are really working for two separate international markets for manufacturers: among the developed countries, trade would be unimpeded except by tariffs; but imports into the rich world from developing countries would be restrained, in each industry, to a fixed proportion of internal demand. This extreme version of protectionism is unlikely to happen, he says, adding:

> The world may yet get an intermediate trade system, liberal in outline, though spotted with hopefully temporary and self-cancelling quantitative restrictions. But it should be aware that each degree by which that system deviated from the liberal norm would impose, for the benefit of very few, a very large cost on the populations of both developed and developing areas.

Those words were written before the world had sunk so deeply into recession. Is the optimism which is implicit in them justified, now that even the richer countries are desperately anxious about their economic futures? Certainly, the pressures for protection are growing stronger, as more and more men and women are thrown out of work in industrialised countries. The fear as I write, in the autumn of 1975, is that the oil battle set off two years ago is only the beginning of a long series of confrontations between producer and consumer nations, extending into a more general warfare between the entrenched, increasingly defence-minded countries of the OECD and those in the Third World.

The danger of that battle-line, however, is causing many people to have second thoughts. Among statesmen in the Third World, it is being accepted that words are less

important than deeds and spirit; that international declarations and treaties are ultimately not enforceable (as the
oil producers demonstrated when they defied UN declarations forbidding economic coercion); and that persuasion
and the creation of common interest are the only rational
means of making progress in international affairs, particularly
those affecting trade.

At the Seventh Special Session of the UN, the New
International Economic Order was shorn of some of the
ideological overtones, which the Americans and others found
so hard to swallow. (One US statement still referred to it as
'something called a New International Economic Order'.) The
reason was a new belief among the more moderate leaders in
the developing countries that the West was now willing to
come to some sensible accord over such problems as
commodities and freer trade in manufactures, and to grant
more concessionary finance for development, when it could
find the money.

Belatedly, the Third World began to see that all such
progress would be imperilled, as it already has been, if the
West was driven deeper into economic recession and recession
of the spirit. It seemed possible, just possible, that the world
was not determined to punish itself by too narrow a pursuit
of supposed self-interest. But no one could be sure. It is
ironic to remember now that more than a decade ago, at
UNCTAD I, the rich world was offered a deal on oil. The
offer was laughed out of court. Have we learned anything
since then?

The spirit of New York in September 1975 gave some
hope that we have. No problems were solved, but one trend
may have been arrested and another trend begun. Up till the
Seventh Special Session, the Third World had been led by a
group of nations — Algeria, Iraq, Libya, Tanzania and
Venezuela among them — whose policy seemed to be to ask
for the moon, and take nothing less. This produced in the
West a parallel group of hawks, consisting of the United
States, Germany and Japan, which was inclined to advise
holding on to set positions and taking no notice of the whole
aggressive stance of the poor countries.

But throughout 1975, attitudes in the EEC and the OECD

were softening. The result was some position papers from the rich countries which aimed at making progress, at the various international gatherings, on subjects where progress seemed possible. After the New York meeting, a British official told me with delight: 'What we hoped would happen did happen. The radicals in the Third World were talked down. They abandoned their commitment to wholesale restructuring of the world (which would not happen), and adopted a piecemeal approach.' This was from a man whose dedication to real changes that will benefit the Third World was not to be doubted.

An Asian delegate confirmed the change of mood:

Sentiment among many of my colleagues towards the United States is becoming more sober, less emotionally hostile. That's why the extremists were defeated in our caucuses and we started talking business with the Americans. The majority in the Third World group didn't want an ideological showdown or political victories, but practical short-term solutions to the real problems.

If these analyses of what happened are right, a new and hopeful trend may indeed have begun. What the Americans, in particular, were anxious to do was to reject the Western guilt which is implicit in the New International Economic Order. This was important to them not only for psychological reasons, but because they felt that to acknowledge the guilt would give the Third World an implied right to punitive confiscation of Western assets. But by claiming that they were willing to make further practical contributions to Third World development, the United States and its allies encouraged the moderates among the developing countries to settle for practical progress, rather than ringing declarations and denunciations.

As ever, the proof of the pie will be in the eating — or in the failing to eat. The tone of the international conferences of 1976, particularly UNCTAD IV in Nairobi and the ILO's World Employment Conference in Geneva, will tell us much about how attitudes are going to develop. The West must soon indicate that, as it begins to climb out of recession, a major share of the fruits of the new success will go to the poorest people on earth. Neither in conscience nor in self-interest can we afford to be niggardly.